Teaching in Blended Learning Environments

T0345318

Issues in Distance Education

Series Editors: Terry Anderson and David Wiley

Distance education is the fastest-growing mode of formal and informal teaching, training, and learning. Its many variants include e-learning, mobile learning, and immersive learning environments. The series presents recent research results and offers informative and accessible overviews, analyses, and explorations of current issues and the technologies and services used in distance education. Each volume focuses on critical questions and emerging trends, while also taking note of the evolutionary history and roots of this specialized mode of education and training. The series is aimed at a wide group of readers including distance education teachers, trainers, administrators, researchers, and students.

SERIES TITLES

Theory and Practice of Online Learning, second edition
edited by Terry Anderson

Mobile Learning: Transforming the Delivery of Education and Training
edited by Mohamed Ally

A Designer's Log: Case Studies in Instructional Design
by Michael Power

Accessible Elements: Teaching Science Online and at a Distance
edited by Dietmar Kennepohl and Lawton Shaw

Emerging Technologies in Distance Education
edited by George Veletsianos

Flexible Pedagogy, Flexible Practice:
Notes from the Trenches of Distance Education
edited by Elizabeth Burge, Chère Campbell Gibson, and Terry Gibson

Teaching in Blended Learning Environments:
Creating and Sustaining Communities of Inquiry
by Norman D. Vaughan, Martha Cleveland-Innes and D. Randy Garrison

TEACHING IN BLENDED LEARNING ENVIRONMENTS

CREATING AND SUSTAINING COMMUNITIES OF INQUIRY

Norman D. Vaughan
Martha Cleveland-Innes
and
D. Randy Garrison

AU PRESS

Copyright © 2013 Norman D. Vaughan, Martha Cleveland-Innes, and D. Randy Garrison

Published by AU Press, Athabasca University
1200, 10011 – 109 Street, Edmonton, AB T5J 3S6

ISBN 978-1-927356-47-0 (print) 978-1-927356-48-7 (PDF) 978-1-927356-49-4 (epub)

Cover and interior design by Sergiy Kozakov.
Printed in Canada.

Library and Archives Canada Cataloguing in Publication

Vaughan, Norman D., 1960-

    Teaching in blended learning environments : creating and sustaining communities of inquiry / Norman D. Vaughan, Martha Cleveland-Innes, and D. Randy Garrison

(Issues in distance education series)
Includes bibliographical references and index.
Issued also in electronic formats.

ISBN 978-1-927356-47-0

    1. Education, Higher—Computer-assisted instruction. 2. Teaching—Computer network resources. 3. Blended learning. 4. Internet in higher education. I. Cleveland-Innes, M. II. Garrison, D. R. (Donn Randy) III. Title. IV. Series: Issues in distance education series.

LB2395.7.V39 2013   371.3   C2013-901785-2

We acknowledge the financial support of the Government of Canada through the Canada Book Fund (CBF) for our publishing activities.

Assistance provided by the Government of Alberta, Alberta Multimedia Development Fund.

Contents

List of Tables

List of Figures

This book is dedicated to our families
who supported our work on this text.

Preface

The focus of this book is the teaching practices required of blended learning approaches and designs in higher education. Our previous book, *Blended Learning in Higher Education* (Garrison & Vaughan, 2008), in which we defined *blended learning* as "the organic integration of thoughtfully selected and complementary face-to-face and online approaches and technologies" (p. 148) guides us in this goal. Feedback from the publication of this first book indicated that the unique feature of this work was the provision of a coherent framework in which to explore the transformative concept of blended learning. Invariably, as we made presentations and conducted workshops, the consistent message we received was about how valuable the rationale is to understanding the purpose and practical challenges of adopting blended learning approaches in higher education. In *Teaching in Blended Learning Environments: Creating and Sustaining Communities of Inquiry*, we build upon the framework and concepts of our previous work.

The context of this book is the growing demand for improved teaching in higher education. Traditionally, faculty members served as content experts, selecting disciplinary content to be transmitted to students largely through lectures. Unfortunately, most faculty members do so with limited knowledge of pedagogy and appreciation of the value and growing importance of engagement in a community of inquiry. This book provides a coherent and comprehensive practical view of teaching in higher education that provides a map of the future in terms of integrating face-to-face and online learning.

Our focus here is on teaching as it relates to the design, facilitation, direction, and assessment of blended learning in contemporary higher education. The transformative innovation of virtual communication and online learning communities creates new ways for teachers and students to engage, interact, and contribute to learning. This new learning environment, when combined with face-to-face interactions, will necessitate significant role adjustments and the need to understand the concept of teaching presence for deep and meaningful learning outcomes. This book defines *teaching presence* as the effort and activity around the design, facilitation, and direction of cognitive and social processes in learning communities for the purpose of realizing personally meaningful and educationally worthwhile learning.

Introducing a phenomenon as complex as teaching presence in a blended learning context is a daunting task. Beyond discussing teaching with technology, writing this book was a process of explicating, examining, and describing a very different approach to higher education — an approach that represents the era of blended learning. We see that "neither the purpose, the methods, nor the population for whom education is intended today, bear any resemblance to those on which formal education is historically based" (Pond, 2002, n.p.). These changes include a new way of conceiving of, and offering, teaching and learning. The need for, and purpose of, this book lies in the fact that the context, the technology, and the students that are part of contemporary higher education are different, and those differences must be accommodated in the teaching practices of our institutions (Dziuban et al., 2010).

To make these changes relevant and real, the book focuses on the practice of teaching in blended learning environments. In addition to addressing new approaches to teaching and learning in higher education, two central ideas come together. First, information and communications technology provide the opportunity to create communities of learners that support engagement and collaboration. The online Community of Inquiry theoretical framework introduced by Garrison, Anderson, and Archer (2000) guides this idea. The reason their framework is valuable for this task is the active presence of a teacher at its core, working toward active cognitive and social presence of all the participants. Distinguished from the lecturer transmitting accepted knowledge in traditional face-to-face teaching ("sage on the stage"), or the role of instructor in traditional distance education ("guide on the side"), the teacher in a blended environment is collaboratively present in designing, facilitating, and directing the educational experience.

The second idea that illuminates teaching presence in blended learning environments is defining *principles of practice*. We define seven principles that reflect the realities of new and emerging information and communications technologies. Moreover, it is important to recognize that "just blending face-to-face learning with information technologies cannot provide effective teaching and efficient solutions for learning" (Hadjerrouit, 2008, p. 29). The need to go beyond capricious blending of face-to-face and online activities is revealed in the importance of these principles to allow us to capitalize on the potential of information and communication technologies. These principles provide the organizational structure to this book.

It takes more than adjusted face-to-face principles of teaching (see Chickering & Gamson, 1987) to harness all the opportunities for teaching and learning available through technology. Principles of practice intended to develop teaching presence in blended learning communities must account for new, emerging possibilities and roles. This book offers new principles of teaching presence for blended learning designs in higher education. The seven principles emerge out of the requirements of a collaborative community of inquiry, where learning is situated in purposeful inquiry and where students collaboratively assume shared responsibility and control to design, facilitate, and direct inquiry. The seven principles, and the concepts that provide their foundation, are explored across the next seven chapters of this book.

In the introductory chapter we describe blending learning, define the Community of Inquiry (CoI) theoretical framework that shapes the structure of this book, and outline the seven principles of blended learning that provide the inspiration for the practical guidelines and suggestions that constitute the primary contribution of this book. Successful blended learning is dependent upon the creation of a collaborative community of inquiry and an understanding of the principles of teaching presence that guides, engages, and successfully achieves a worthwhile educational experience.

Chapter 2 describes the first phase of teaching presence: the design and organization of a collaborative community of inquiry. It focuses on the coherent integration of curriculum, climate, active tasks and assignments, timelines, and assessment rubrics. This chapter provides a description of successful case studies and examples that maximize the critical discourse and reflective potential of blended learning methods and techniques.

Chapter 3 explores the social and cognitive principles of facilitation. Facilitation goes to the core of the dynamics of a community of inquiry. Collaborative communities emerge, and are sustained, through shared purpose, joint activity, and interaction. These commonalities must be identified, illuminated, and fostered through the teacher's leadership in order to facilitate these aspects of community. Social presence emerges and cognitive presence evolves through facilitation. Facilitating social interaction fosters social presence, which is central to setting the stage for continued collaborative activity. However, pushing beyond social interaction to critical discourse moves cognitive presence to deep and meaningful learning. Strategies for the facilitation of social and cognitive presence are described in terms of practical examples.

Chapter 4 speaks to the use of direct instruction. This involves helping students to manage collaborative relationships in order to assume increasing responsibility for their learning and ensuring that students move toward resolution in their course-based discussions and assignments. Direct instruction is about academic and pedagogic leadership; it is educational leadership that provides disciplinary focus and structure and scaffolding but also offers students the choice and opportunity to assume increasing responsibility for their learning. This instruction is more than a "guide on the side," but less than a "sage on the stage." It is an approach where learning is socially shared. This is the path to a meaningful, systematic, and worthwhile educational experience. Students remain engaged and focused while achieving desired learning outcomes. This chapter provides practical guidelines and strategies for directing social and cognitive presence in a blended learning environment.

Chapter 5 addresses the final principle regarding assessment. Educational researchers (Thistlethwaite, 2006; Hedberg & Corrent-Agostinho, 1999) state that assessment drives learning in higher education. The design of assessment activity and feedback influence the type of learning that takes place (Entwistle, 2000). The purpose of this chapter is to demonstrate the types of self-reflection, peer feedback, and teacher-directed assessment techniques that can be used to support a blended community of inquiry approach to learning in higher education.

Chapter 6 provides a discussion of digital technologies and instructional strategies that can be used to design collaborative communities of inquiry. This chapter reiterates the interdependent elements of social, cognitive, and teaching presence and provides corresponding social media application examples and associated collaborative learning activities. Educational strategies for using these tools to support a collaborative community of inquiry, in a blended learning environment, are illustrated and discussed.

Chapter 7 concludes the book with a summary of key ideas and strategies for teaching in a blended teaching format.

Overall, the book is a coherent view of the principles for the integration of face-to-face and online learning made explicit. Second, the book is grounded in the actual practice of blended learning.

CONCLUSION

The primary audience for this book is college faculty and graduate students interested in quality teaching in blended learning environments. The secondary audience is education technology professionals, instructional designers, teaching and learning developers, and instructional aides — all those involved in the design and development of the media and materials for blended learning. Other audiences include higher education administrators, education researchers, and government officials interested in quality education issues. While focused primarily on blended learning in higher education, the principles can be easily adjusted for application in the K–12 environment and the workplace.

1 Conceptual Framework

The community of inquiry is perhaps the most promising methodology for the encouragement of that fusion of critical and creative
cognitive processing known as higher-order thinking. (Lipman, 1991,
p. 204)

INTRODUCTION

Blended learning has received increasing attention with the infusion
of web-based technologies into the learning and teaching process.
Virtually all courses in higher education incorporate information
and communication technologies to some degree. These technologies create new opportunities for students to interact with their
peers, faculty, and content. The infusion of information and communications technology in higher education draws attention to the
theory and practice of blended learning.

Blended learning inherently demands a fundamental rethinking of the educational experience and presents a challenge to traditional presentational approaches. If we are to deal with the theoretical and practical complexities of rethinking the educational experience from a blended learning perspective, then the first challenge is to provide a conceptual order that goes beyond rigid recipes. Such order and coherence is of particular importance for practitioners who may not have a full appreciation of the possibilities that new and emerging technologies present for engaging learners in innovative educational experiences. It seems to us that a conceptual framework may well be of the utmost practical value to assist practitioners to navigate through the educational and technological levels of complexity.

The purpose of this chapter is to describe blended learning briefly and then to establish the rationale through which we can explore the practical challenges in implementing blended learning approaches in higher education. This rationale is operationalized in the Community of Inquiry (CoI) theoretical framework (Garrison, 2011). The Community of Inquiry framework is outlined with a particular focus on teaching presence. From this framework are derived the seven principles of blended learning that shape the structure of this book.

BLENDED LEARNING DESCRIBED

While it is clear to most that the core of blended learning is the integration of face-to-face and online learning activities, it is important to recognize that simply adding an online component does not necessarily meet the threshold of blended learning as defined here. In the book that set the stage for this work, *Blended Learning in Higher Education*, we provided a succinct definition of *blended learning* as "the organic integration of thoughtfully selected and complementary face-to-face and online approaches" (Garrison & Vaughan, 2008, p. 148). By *organic* we meant grounded in practice, and by the use of the term *thoughtfully*, we wanted to indicate a significant rethinking of how we should be approaching the learning experience.

With regard to a thoughtful approach, we specifically excluded enhancing traditional practices that do not significantly improve student engagement. That said, we do not want to restrict innovative blended learning designs by providing strict parameters as to the percentage of time spent face-to-face or online. We have chosen to provide a qualitative definition, which distinguishes blended learning as an approach that addresses the educational needs of the course or program through a thoughtful fusion of the best and most appropriate face-to-face and online activities. The key is to avoid, at all costs, simply layering on activities and responsibilities until the course is totally unmanageable and students do not have the time to reflect on meaning and engage in discourse for shared understanding.

Blended learning is the inspiration of much of the innovation, both pedagogically and technologically, in higher education. By *innovation* we mean significantly rethinking and redesigning approaches to teaching and learning that fully engage learners. The essential function of blended learning is to extend thinking and discourse over time and space. There is considerable rhetoric in higher education about the importance of engagement, but most institutions' dominant mode of delivery remains delivering content either through the lecture or self-study course modules. Blended learning is specifically directed to enhancing engagement through the innovative adoption of purposeful online learning activities.

The strength of integrating face-to-face synchronous communication and text-based online asynchronous communication is powerfully complementary for higher educational purposes. The goal of blended learning is to bring these together to academically challenge students in ways not possible through either mode individually. There is a distinct multiplier effect when integrating verbal and written modes of communication. An added benefit is that blended learning sustains academic communication over time.

Moreover, students have time to reflect and respond thoughtfully. Finally, while significant administrative advantages are gained through blended learning designs (access, retention, campus space, teaching resources), the focus here is the quality of the learning experience made possible though blended learning approaches.

In the next section we explore the ideas of engagement and academic inquiry central to the ideals of higher education. These ideas are inherent to learning communities and provide the foundation for implementing blended learning. Learning communities provide the conditions for discussion, negotiation, and agreement in face-to-face and online environments with virtually limitless possibilities to connect to others and to information. Such a community, which we describe next, frames the principles that shape this book.

COMMUNITY OF INQUIRY

Lipman (1991) has argued that education is inquiry. He suggests, "The community of inquiry is perhaps the most promising methodology for the encouragement of that fusion of critical and creative cognitive processing known as higher-order thinking" (Lipman, 1991, p. 204). Critical thinking is most often cited as the hallmark of higher education. Therefore, we view a community of inquiry as the concept that best captures the ideal of a higher educational experience. Our belief is that practitioners can create the conditions for critical thinking, rational judgments, and understanding through the engagement of a community of inquiry. Both a sense of community and a commitment to the process of inquiry must be in place.

The Community of Inquiry (CoI) theoretical framework is unique in framing our discussion of the practical implications of blended learning in higher education. It has been the focus of extensive study and validation for over a decade (Garrison, 2011). The premise of the CoI framework is that higher education is both a collaborative and an individually constructivist learning experience. As such, we have this seemingly paradoxical but essential connection between cognitive independence and social interdependence. We argue that personal reflection and shared discourse are requisite for higher learning and, practically, are best realized in an educational community of inquiry. A community of inquiry is where "students listen to one another with respect, build on one another's ideas, challenge one another to supply reasons for otherwise unsupported opinions, assist each other in drawing inferences from what has been said, and seek to identify one another's assumptions" (Lipman, 2003, p. 20).

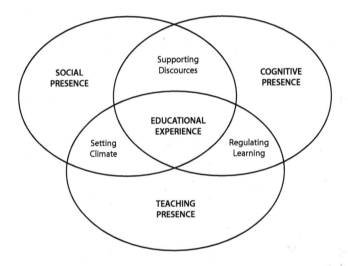

FIGURE 1.1. Community of Inquiry framework

The three key elements or dimensions of the CoI framework are social, cognitive, and teaching presence (Figure 1.1). It is at the convergence of these three mutually reinforcing elements that a collaborative constructivist educational experience is realized. Social presence creates the environment for trust, open communication, and group cohesion. *Cognitive presence* has been defined "as the extent to which learners are able to construct and confirm meaning through sustained reflection and discourse in a critical community of inquiry" (Garrison, Anderson, & Archer, 2001, p. 11). It has been operationalized through the developmental phases of inquiry — a triggering event, exploration, integration, and resolution. The third and cohesive element, teaching presence, is associated with the design, facilitation, and direction of a community of inquiry. This unifying force brings together the social and cognitive processes directed to personally meaningful and educationally worthwhile outcomes.

ELEMENTS	CATEGORIES	INDICATORS (examples only)
Social Presence	Personal/Affective Open Communication Group Cohesion	Self projection/expressing emotions Learning climate/risk-free expression Group identity/collaboration
Cognitive Presence	Triggering Event Exploration Integration Resolution	Sense of puzzlement Information exchange Connecting ideas Applying new ideas
Teaching Presence	Design & Organization Facilitating Discourse Direct Instruction	Setting curriculum & methods Shaping constructive exchange Focusing and resolving issues

FIGURE 1.2. Community of Inquiry categories and indicators

To assist in gaining a greater appreciation of the categories of each of the presences (Figure 1.2), we provide indicators and examples of meaningful activities associated with each presence. A quality, blended community of inquiry should reflect these activities. It is important to appreciate each category and its progressive or developmental nature. For example, teaching presence begins with a design phase and then progresses to facilitation and direct instruction to ensure the successful resolution of the problem or task. This cycle will repeat throughout a course of studies. The developmental and cyclical nature of each of the presences is perhaps more obvious within cognitive presence and its phases of inquiry. Social presence also has a developmental progression. The first goal in establishing social presence is to recognize the need for identity with the purpose (academic goal) and not to focus too strongly on interpersonal relationships. Interpersonal relationships can and should develop over time, while issues of open communication and group cohesion must be the primary focus at the beginning of the inquiry process (Garrison, 2011).

TEACHING PRESENCE

Introducing a phenomenon as complex as teaching presence in a blended learning context is a daunting task. Beyond discussing teaching with technology, this task requires explicating, examining, and describing a new approach to teaching in a new era of higher education. We see that required changes in higher education are now emergent, for "neither the purpose, the methods, nor the population for whom education is intended today, bear any resemblance to those on which formal education is historically based" (Pond, 2002, para. 2). These changes include a new way of conceiving of, and offering, teaching and learning.

We focus here on the teaching presence construct as growing evidence points to the importance of teaching presence for the success of a community of inquiry (Akyol & Garrison, 2008; Arbaugh, 2008; Eom, 2006; Shea, Li, Swan, & Pickett, 2005). The conceptual framework we offer requires new ways of thinking about the role of teacher and the role of student. Blended learning provides expanded possibilities and difficult choices for the educator and participants in a community of inquiry. The responsibilities of teaching presence are distributed within the learning community but are not diminished; the importance and challenge is only magnified. Teaching presence is enhanced when participants become more metacognitively aware and are encouraged to assume increasing responsibility and control of their learning. Much attention needs to be focused on teaching presence if we are to create and sustain the conditions for higher order learning.

This issue of shared responsibility makes the point that each participant in a community of inquiry must take some responsibility for social, cognitive, and teaching presence. This is why the third element is labeled *teaching* presence and not *teacher* presence. It is not just the teacher who is responsible for social and cognitive presence issues. All participants in a collaborative learning environment must assume various degrees of teaching responsibilities depending on the specific content, developmental level, and ability. From a cognitive presence perspective, instructor and students must be prepared to clarify expectations, negotiate requirements, engage in critical discourse, diagnose misconceptions, and assess understanding. Participants must also be aware of social presence issues and ensure that everybody feels that they belong and is comfortable contributing to the discourse but also prepared to challenge ideas respectfully.

The pioneering innovation of virtual communication and community requires both teacher and student to engage, interact, and contribute to learning in new ways. The challenge is that simply providing opportunities for interaction and collaboration does not provide assurance that students will approach their learning in deep and meaningful ways. The role of learner in blended learning environments constitutes multiple roles and responsibilities. This creates role complexity, as participants must assume varying degrees of responsibility to monitor and regulate the dynamics of the learning community. This is consistent with the very nature of a community of inquiry with shared academic goals and processes.

Moving beyond the premise of shared responsibility, what requirements are embodied in the art of teaching in a blended learning environment? First, teaching presence must be true to the learning objectives of the subject while attending to the needs and capabilities students bring to the experience. However, the ways in which the role of effective teaching is crafted in blended learning environments are different and more complex. We create a clear picture of the role of effective teaching in blended higher education that creates the conditions for deep and meaningful learning. As this occurs, change will occur in the classroom, shifting what is done there as well. As we illuminate and reconstruct the process of teaching in higher education through the creation of blended learning communities, we must also examine the assumptions of teaching, the practices common to all teaching delivery in higher education, the new roles for teacher and student that emerge from these changes, the principles appropriate to the combination of teaching face-to-face and online, and the relevant changes to assessment strategies.

PRINCIPLES

Principles are essential to the translation of theoretical frameworks into coherent practical strategies and techniques. Principles become even more valuable when coping with the complexities of integrating the potential of new and emerging communications technology. While the principles of good practice associated with the traditional classroom have generic value, they do not adequately consider the collaborative constructivist approaches and communication technologies being adopted in higher education.

A principled approach to teaching that emerges from a sustained community of inquiry takes us beyond the traditional lecture all too common in higher education. The principles that shape this book and give structure to teaching presence encourage students to assume greater responsibility and control of their educational experience. To help put the principles discussed here into context, we begin with a brief examination of the most prominent set of teaching and learning principles in higher education. Those are the widely cited and adopted principles of good practice in undergraduate education published by Chickering and Gamson (1987). These principles are as follows:

1. Encourage contact between students and faculty.
2. Develop reciprocity and cooperation among students.
3. Encourage active learning.
4. Give prompt feedback.
5. Emphasize time on task.
6. Communicate high expectations.
7. Respect diverse talents and ways of learning.

The Chickering and Gamson principles were generated from research on teaching and learning and have guided educational practice in higher education over the last two decades. They were, however, based on traditional practice, which focused largely on the lecture, and were generated and intended for face-to-face environments. Moreover, they were formulated through consensus in a largely atheoretical manner. These principles are too often interpreted as a means to improve the lecture format, which is not necessarily how we can better engage learners in more active and collaborative educational experiences.

While these principles have served higher education well in directing attention to good teaching and learning practice, we believe that these principles need to be updated to address the changing needs in higher education to become information literate in the age of the Internet. These principles must be consistent with the ubiquitous connectivity afforded students today. It is time to create a new set of principles that can better reflect the ideals of a higher education experience by recognizing and utilizing the capabilities of new and emerging information and communications technologies. While these principles are not incongruent with blended learning environments, there are conditions, assumptions, and properties of technologically mediated learning environments that require an update of these principles.

Collaborative constructivist approaches are more than interaction and engagement. As valuable as the principles of contact, cooperation, active learning, feedback, time on task, and respect are, the collaborative approaches and principles discussed here address new requirements of the knowledge age of the 21st century. The educational approaches needed today represent purposeful collaboration to resolve an issue, solve a problem, or create new understandings. The educational process outlined here is situated in the context of a community of learners focused on purposeful inquiry where students collaboratively assume increased responsibility and control to resolve specific problems and issues.

The seven principles that shape this book are deductively derived from the CoI theoretical framework. The principles are organized around the three sub-elements or categories of teaching presence: design, facilitation, and direction. Within each of these three functions and areas of responsibility, we address the elements of social and cognitive presence. Considering the complexity of a collaborative blended learning experience, considerable care and thought must be devoted to design, facilitation, and direction.

The following principles provide a map and guide to creating and sustaining purposeful communities of inquiry:

1. Plan for the creation of open communication and trust.
2. Plan for critical reflection and discourse.
3. Establish community and cohesion.
4. Establish inquiry dynamics (purposeful inquiry).
5. Sustain respect and responsibility.
6. Sustain inquiry that moves to resolution.
7. Ensure assessment is congruent with intended processes and outcomes.

The first two principles speak to the social and cognitive challenge of designing a collaborative blended learning experience. The next two principles address the social and cognitive concerns associated with facilitating a community of inquiry. The last three deal with the social, cognitive, and assessment responsibilities of directing an educational experience to achieve the desired outcomes successfully. These seven principles are the first step in providing specific practical guidelines to the design, facilitation, and direction of a collaborative community of inquiry.

CONCLUSION

The challenge now is to explore systematically the strategies and techniques where we can fuse face-to-face and online learning that will create purposeful communities of inquiry in the support of deep and meaningful approaches to teaching and learning. We need to explore the strengths and weaknesses of face-to-face and online experiences as we consider each of these principles. This will be done in subsequent chapters, which will focus on the design, facilitation, direction, and assessment of blended learning experiences.

2 Design

Appreciating teaching presence is an enormous design challenge but crucial if we are to avoid the potential anarchy of the Internet and the "cult of the amateur." (Keen, 2007, p.3)

INTRODUCTION

How can we design a community of inquiry that includes interaction and collaboration in a blended learning environment? The following discussion will direct the instructor to key design elements that are essential for realizing the potential of a blended learning course. The design principles explored here will guide instructors in the design and delivery of an engaging and collaborative blended learning course.

There is, however, a caveat to our discussion. We believe the instructor ultimately has control and responsibility for the design and delivery of an educational experience. At the same time, the

Internet and communications technology have "flattened" the educational world and provided enormous possibilities for learner choice, flexibility, and interaction. This flattening of the educational environment should not, however, translate into a diminution of educational responsibility. Appreciating teaching presence is an enormous design challenge but a crucial one if we are to avoid the potential anarchy of the Internet and the "cult of the amateur" (Keen, 2007). To allow the unpredictable influence of the Internet to undermine teaching presence would be a grave mistake if the goals are discourse, critical reflection, and deep understanding.

Our central contemporary educational challenge is how we design purposeful educational experiences using the potential of the Internet to bring teachers and learners together in sustained ways, while not losing the focus and direction central to any educational experience. More specifically, how do we design an educational experience that combines the potential for asynchronous online and synchronous face-to-face discourse in a reflective manner that provides the time to think deeply and not speed over enormous amounts of content? How do educators balance the flexibility and freedom of online learning with the expert guidance found in a purposeful face-to-face learning environment? We address blended course design and challenges in this chapter. The central challenge of blended designs rests on the thoughtful combination of the Internet and the culture of critical inquiry in higher education.

Adding on to excessive workloads or simply reducing class time will not meet the need for more meaningful learning experiences in this age of access to copious amounts of information via the Internet. Nor will we see any improvements in learning satisfaction or in outcomes through faculty development workshops that work on the margins by promoting the latest techniques. If we hope to make significant gains in the quality of the educational experience, which must be the goal as the educational needs of society are changing so radically, then we must focus on fundamental redesign strategies. Design is central to releasing the potential of blended learning and is the focus of this chapter.

INSTRUCTIONAL DESIGN

Design is a planning process that includes consideration of many content and process issues related to the intended learning outcomes. The planning process described here is shaped at the conceptual level by assumptions, principles, and purposes. Design begins, prior to course commencement, with a holistic perspective describing the assumptions and approaches to learning. This then provides a framework for principles and guidelines that shape the design process of choosing content, creating student learning activities of collaboration and interaction, and identifying assessment procedures. Thoughtful instructional design is guided by this framework, which provides direction regarding content and process decision points. This broad approach is important; simply focusing on content provides little direction with regard to the process of constructing knowledge. Design will have a pragmatic impact on how students approach learning (Garrison & Cleveland-Innes, 2005).

The planning process is further shaped at a practical level by educational and technical possibilities and constraints. Paying attention to these conceptual and practical elements is another challenge in design. The goal is to find a solution with the least compromise to a collaborative community of learners engaged in purposeful educational activities. The design approach described in this chapter is to focus on the educational goals and strategies and let them determine the instructional technologies that are possible and appropriate for the purpose. The design process is to bring into alignment the goals of education with the properties of the technology.

Flexibility is a key design consideration. In an educational context, design is a process that constructs a flexible plan, one that must be open to the unexpected and allow for change of direction while staying within the parameters of the educational goals. Design must not be deterministic and rigid. Design is shaped by instructional theory, but evolving conditions during implementation necessitate instructional decisions. As circumstances change (as they inevitably will) and expectations are negotiated, design adjusts. As such, design and implementation must not be separated. Design continues during the implementation phase. The instructor is also a course designer (unlike the industrial approaches of mega-distance education institutions), necessitating that an instructor have both content and pedagogical expertise. An instructional design should be a resource, an important resource, yet one that is open to modification by an instructor with the experience and judgment to achieve the intended educational goals efficiently.

The educational experience is a complex and dynamic process that will inevitably produce unexpected results. Design must be sufficiently flexible to allow considerable customization to meet the educational needs of a specific group of learners. To help manage this complexity, designers and instructors need principles to guide design and implementation decisions. The principles that shape the community of inquiry are grounded in a collaborative constructivist view of learning. The quality of the instructional design will depend upon these principles. These principles, outlined in chapter 1, go beyond using technology to access and deliver content. We recognize that what is learned is inseparable from how it is learned. The issue (as it has always been in higher education) is to design the educational transaction that will engage learners in purposeful and collaborative activities that support discourse and reflection. In this regard, technology is an enabler: instructional design that fosters collaborative engagement is the first challenge if we are to achieve worthwhile educational processes and outcomes.

Often the challenge is to redesign a course or program of studies to gain effectiveness, efficiency, and flexibility in a blended learning context. This demands an evaluation of the current design from the perspective of engagement, collaboration, and community. Deficiencies (e. g., interaction) and constraints (e.g., nature of the content) associated with the current design must be critically analyzed and new perspectives considered. Ultimately, the instructor and designer (often the same person) will determine the end product. The Community of Inquiry conceptual framework can be enormously helpful in doing so (Vaughan, 2010a).

In summary, reaching the potential of blended learning necessitates a thoughtful investment in the design process. Thoughtfully integrating face-to-face and computer-mediated approaches introduces the need for explicit instructional design. This represents a considerable challenge, which will be amply rewarded in terms of the quality of the educational experience. Every expectation is that this more rigorous design process will make greater use of deep approaches to learning and result in higher levels of cognitive presence (Shea & Bidjerano, 2009). What must be avoided is an incremental design approach—simply layering additional activities, such as a discussion board—onto a full course of studies that employs a deficient approach to teaching and learning (e.g., a lecture). This can only lead to frustration, dissatisfaction, and diminished learning outcomes.

Best practices that are applicable to all blended learning course designs are not available. The possibilities and variations that could be classified as blended learning do not allow for generalized best practices. For this reason, we have organized our discussion of teaching presence around a set of seven principles derived from a framework consistent with the ideals of higher education. The CoI framework is the genesis of these principles that frame this book. In this chapter we focus on the first two principles—the design of social presence and the design of cognitive presence. While we treat each of the presences and principles separately for purposes of reducing complexity, we must keep in mind that there is considerable overlap of the presences, and suggestions for one will address issues for the other.

SOCIAL PRESENCE

Designing a blended or online learning experience requires considerable attention and effort prior to the start of the course. This is because we are trying to fuse two very different but complementary modes of communication and interaction. We are challenged to blend synchronous and asynchronous communication functionally, in a way that will be congruent with the educational goals and contextual constraints. This means making informed design decisions among an enormously broad range of educational activities and media. Considerable attention is required at the design stage for blended learning. However, taking the time to create a thoughtful, coherent course structure will see a pay-off in time and effort saved during the delivery of the course and in realizing intended goals. While great benefits are realized in a blended teaching and learning experience, it does take considerable time and effort, particularly in the initial design stage, on the part of instructors.

The first design principle, identified below, focuses on social presence. Social presence, as defined in chapter 1, is not just a "feel good" issue. Social presence sets the environmental conditions for higher learning. Research has shown social presence to be an essential mediating variable between teaching presence and cognitive presence (Garrison, Cleveland-Innes, & Fung, 2010; Shea & Bidjerano, 2009). Social presence is connected to perceived learning and persistence (Akyol & Garrison, 2008; Boston et al., 2009) and the academic goals of an educational experience by supporting a questioning and reflective predisposition and creating a secure climate for critical discourse.

PRINCIPLE: *Plan to establish a climate that will support open communication and cohesion.*

Establishing and sustaining a community of learners is the focus of the first principle. First, attention must be given to affective concerns in order to create the conditions for open communication, cohesion, and interpersonal connections. In creating these conditions, social presence then links directly to cognitive presence and learning. All the presences are interdependent and influence each other. The focus of social presence is to support the affect, communication, interpersonal connections, and cohesion that support the inquiry process and deep approaches to learning required for cognitive presence.

The design strategy used here has three elements: organization, delivery, and assessment. Each of the design elements are implemented to support the principle described above.

ORGANIZATION

The organizational structure of a course must consider social presence and the dynamics of establishing trust as a foundation for open communication and group cohesion. Building trust must begin even before the first class. Trust is built by removing the unknowns about other group members. For example, the group becomes more familiar by having all group members provide short bios. This can be done verbally in the face-to-face classroom, virtually in the online classroom, or both. During the first class, students should be given time for interaction with other students and the instructor in order to decrease ambiguity about group members and the instructor, increase trust, and begin to develop relationships. Small group introductory exercises, for introductions to each other and the content, provide this opportunity.

It becomes quickly apparent during the organizational phase that group cohesion may be complicated by contextual contingencies related to technology. Content and activities must be structured and matched to the pedagogical approach and the technology used throughout the course. For example, it is generally recognized that starting with a face-to-face experience can expedite setting climate and developing community. In this regard, when planning the first session the task of discussing expectations and providing introductions will need to be approached in different ways in a face-to-face or online context. In a face-to-face environment, the first session can be organized around small group discussions, exploring expectations and providing opportunities to get acquainted. However, support, direction, and examples should be offered in an online environment, by having participants create a bio page and engage in some preliminary activities that allow students to discuss the course and to get acquainted.

Strategies will then need to be developed through collaborative activities such as discussion boards and assignments to continue to develop group cohesion and common purpose. Collaborative activities build social presence. How are these best initiated and then sustained? A good strategy is to require a group project. Students in a blended course can meet face-to-face or online synchronously, perhaps also using web-based conferencing software such as Adobe Connect or Blackboard Collaborate. The latter is also an opportunity for the instructor to connect with the class between face-to-face sessions. Once students get into a project, an online forum or wiki could be used to construct a presentation or document (Figure 2.1).

Social media technologies are designed to engage Internet users, more so than the initial flat and information-push websites, and they provide enhanced interaction for building and sustaining community development. These ubiquitous technologies provide a range of asynchronous and synchronous online communication tools. The key is to understand the capabilities of these tools in terms of educational goals and objectives, as well as their ability to sustain social presence in a community of inquiry.

FIGURE 2.1. Summary of online discussion forum collaboratively constructed in Wikspaces

The technology is an enabler and provides the means to stay connected and to achieve true collaborative constructivist approaches. Consideration must be given to the effort required to learn to use the technology (from both the instructor and student perspectives) compared to the educational benefit. Table 2.1 provides examples of activities that harness the potential of social media tools in order to establish a climate that will support open communication and cohesion. Additional strategies for using social media applications are further described in chapter 6.

TABLE 2.1. Examples of activities for establishing a climate that will support open communication and cohesion

ACTIVITY	DESCRIPTION
Introductory letter or video clip	Consider composing a letter or creating a YouTube video clip that welcomes students, briefly describes your teaching philosophy, and suggests the role you envision for students in this course. This letter or YouTube clip can then be posted to an introductory discussion forum in a learning management system (e.g., Blackboard) where students can comment on your introduction and also introduce themselves.
Powerful learning experience discussion	On the first day of class, engage your students in an exercise where they each reflect back on an event that was a very powerful learning experience for them – it might or might not have been school related. Have the students, first, individually record their reflections and then form small groups to share their learning experiences and discuss why they were powerful. Debrief as a whole class about what makes learning experiences powerful and relate the discussion to the blended teaching and learning approaches that you have envisioned for your course.
Learning preferences inventory	Ask students to take a learning preferences inventory (a number of them can be found on the Internet) and to reflect on their individual results. "What specific learning strategies and study behaviours will help me succeed in this course?" Individual written reflections can be turned in or posted to a discussion forum or shared in small groups.
Discussion with previous students	Invite a couple of students from a previous class to attend the introductory face-to-face session or join an online discussion to talk about the nature of the course as they experienced it. They can share study approaches they found helpful and generally give suggestions about how to take best advantage of the blended learning environment to be successful in the course.

DELIVERY

When we focus on delivering an educational experience, we go to the heart of a community of inquiry: It speaks to the ideals of a collaborative constructivist educational environment and how we create and sustain purposeful learning activities. Students should be encouraged to develop personal relationships in a forum specifically designed for social sharing (Figure 2.2).

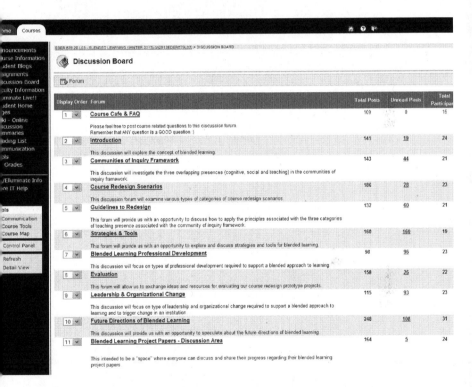

FIGURE 2.2. Course cafe and frequently asked questions (FAQ) discussion forum in the Blackboard learning management system

When we view social presence from a teaching perspective, facilitating open communication and group cohesion are of central importance.

Setting the boundaries of group behaviour accomplishes this. Clear guidelines must be discussed regarding expectations of both classroom and online discussion etiquette. To foster engagement and participation, setting guidelines is best done collaboratively. However, instructors can encourage and require that certain guidelines, if they don't surface from group discussion, be included. The following are examples of guidelines that we use for our online discussions:

1. Do more than state agreement or disagreement. Justify and support your opinion. The most persuasive opinions are supported by evidence, examples, reasons, and facts. If you disagree with something, say why.

2. Do the appropriate preparation, such as reading and class activity work, before you join the discussion.

3. Keep your comments fairly brief. A paragraph or two is plenty unless you are posting something that by nature has to be longer — a short story, for example.

4. Check your message before you send it. Pay attention to your spelling and grammar, and be sure your message makes the points you want to make in a clear and concise way. Remember, other students and instructors can read your messages.

5. Help move the discussion along. When contributing to a discussion, read other people's comments first. Introduce new ideas, but also build on what others have said ("piggyback" on others' ideas).

6. Keep up with the discussion throughout the course. After you have made your contribution on a topic, check back a few times to find out how the discussion is evolving. Does someone's comment make you think twice about your view?

7. Share your experience with your fellow students. You

may be able to offer advice to someone who is new to the course.

8. Respect others' ideas and opinions. Feel free to disagree, but express your disagreement in a respectful manner.

9. Be positive when offering advice. If one of your fellow students posts something to be edited or asks for your opinion on a piece of writing, be encouraging with your comments. If you see weaknesses in someone's writing or ideas, focus on describing the strengths to keep up and the opportunities for improvement. Put yourself in the shoes of the other people in the conference discussions.

10. Be gracious when receiving advice. When you post your work, you are hoping that other people will tell you what you have done well and suggest useful ideas about how to do even better. When others are critical, assume that they are trying to provide a critique, not criticism in the negative sense. Even if they don't seem diplomatic, be gracious in response.

Facilitation by the instructor should be emphasized at the beginning of a discussion topic in order to encourage students to participate. Be aware of a common initial risk: If the instructor dominates the discussion, students may be intimidated and, thereby, discouraged from offering their thoughts. Once students understand the expectations for discussion, the instructor needs to be present but should not dominate. This is critical in the early phases of a discussion in order to model academic discourse. While social presence is crucial, participants must stay focused on the academic objective in a formal discussion topic. Here are some additional strategies to help accomplish this task.

1. Timely instructor attention is meaningful to students. Respond in the face-to-face classroom or online. Model verbal immediacy behaviours in interactions with students and encourage them to do the same.

2. Share your experiences and beliefs in reference to the subject matter with students. Support and encourage students when they provide their own.

3. Course participation has long been left entirely up to the student. Making participation part of the course requirements is valuable online and can be so face-to-face as well. Make participation, in class and online discussion, a significant part of course grades.

4. Instructors can demonstrate engagement and presence by summarizing discussion threads at regular intervals. Once students are engaged and comfortable, have selected students summarize discussion threads.

5. The discussions in online environments are documentation of content and learning and are valuable beyond the process of posting. Encourage students to incorporate materials from the discussions in their assignments.

6. Open communication supports a healthy climate for collaboration, which in turn fosters trust and group cohesion. Design collaborative activities for learning and assessment, such as problem-solving tasks, projects, and small group presentations.

7. Blended environments allow for real-time engagement and interaction. This can be offered online as well; use Internet applications such as chat functions, web-cams, collaborative whiteboards, and interactive video.

In the early stages of delivery for social presence, learners working online need time to feel comfortable communicating in a primarily text-based environment and must adjust to expressing emotion and communicating openly without visual or other context cues. Instructors need to be sensitive and supportive in this regard;

instructor posts set the tone for openness and comfort, in what and how they post (Cleveland-Innes & Garrison, 2009).

The third aspect of design is assessment. While we must consider assessment from a design perspective, assessment is the seventh principle, which we will discuss in depth in chapter 5. At this point we will simply foreshadow a few of the key issues that need to be considered at the design phase.

First, we must distinguish between formative and summative assessment. The purpose of formative assessment is to diagnose misunderstanding and provide constructive feedback and guidance to ensure continued progress. Formative feedback is particularly effective in creating and sustaining social presence. Students must be provided feedback and reinforcement to participate in a community of inquiry. A community of inquiry is a challenging environment, and students must be given feedback with regard to their communication patterns and effectiveness in working collaboratively. As stated earlier, instructor response and attention is the critical piece of this feedback. Where social presence is established, students will be able to identify with the group, feel comfortable engaging in open discourse, and begin to give each other feedback. This demonstrates that trust and group cohesion exist, which is essential if students are to function effectively in a community of inquiry.

We know from the literature on deep learning that educational context, and particularly assessment, has a significant impact on outcomes (Cleveland-Innes & Emes, 2005). Graded activities that require collaboration and constructivist thought will encourage students to work to this end. The activities include group projects, peer assessments, presentations, theory and model building, and structured academic debate.

COGNITIVE PRESENCE

The second design principle focuses on the goal of the educational experience: deep and meaningful learning. The philosophical and theoretical assumptions associated with this approach are grounded in collaborative constructivism. From this perspective, a learner, in collaboration with a community of learners, takes responsibility to construct and confirm meaning. The context and nature of this learning experience is defined by the concept of a community of inquiry and the engagement of all participants in purposeful and disciplined interaction and collaboration. Building this community of inquiry begins by designing for four phases of inquiry – problem definition, exploration, integration, and resolution – through systematic inquiry, discourse, and reflection.

PRINCIPLE: *Plan for activities that support systematic inquiry, discourse and reflection.*

Clear expectations and understanding of the inquiry process should be presented and discussed in the early stages of the course. Then the course activities shift to the requirements and assignments associated with the specific objectives of the educational experience. These activities and assignments include opportunities for critical discourse and reflection. Discussion activities are particularly effective at the problem definition and exploration phase. If the goal is to move the discussion through integration to resolution, a deliberate teaching presence will be required. Assignments that best support inquiry are those that have clear expectations and outcomes (e.g., problem- or case-based). Meta-cognition, or explicit presentation of cognitive process, can be valuable as part of the activity to move through these phases of inquiry. This is often an overlooked component of higher order thinking as reflected in the inquiry approach. Students should be formally introduced to the inquiry process and be expected to monitor their contributions and activities with regard to the task at hand. This process of *learning to learn*, and sharing one's individual story of learning, should be an explicit aspect of the design phase.

Designing a blended learning experience should start with organizing the content and activities. In addition, clear objectives for content and performance expectations will ensure a productive educational experience. To realize this advantage, it is crucial that the course outline, assignments, and grading rubric be posted well before the course begins. One of the great sources of confusion and frustration for students occurs when students are not clear about expectations. For this reason, it is extremely important to plan for the discussion and negotiation of the course outline and expectations at the beginning of the course.

Fundamentally rethinking a course for a blended learning design includes the challenge of covering all the content. As the knowledge base of most fields of study is growing exponentially, it has to be recognized that no one course can possibly cover all content on even the narrowest of topics. The challenge is less about what to leave out than it is how to organize it around the key concepts; therefore, during the design phase, the instructor should focus on key concepts and provide organizational models of the content. This can be done by having students construct their own schema (e.g., concept map) or by the instructor providing the conceptual framework. This will provide the organizational structure that students can use productively to explore more deeply the nuances of the subject. Constructing such schema will provide order and a deeper understanding that will stay with the student. Therefore, think more in terms of the inquiry process, be cognizant of simply transmitting information and avoid the latter.

The corollary to excessive content is excessive workloads. Avoid assignments and activities that are not central to the topic (busy work) or are considered optional. The number of assignments should allow students time to construct personal meaning and confirm it through discourse. Constructing and confirming knowledge is an iterative process between discussion and reflection. It is particularly important to provide students the time to process information, considering that thoughtful written discourse is rigorous and time intensive. Therefore, online discussions cannot be rushed and should be at least a week in length. Another practical matter is to ensure that discussion topics have a clear outcome; otherwise discussion will lose focus and stall at the exploration phase. Finally, it is important to set office hours and let students know how quickly they can expect a response from the instructor. Open communication does not mean that you as an instructor are always present. It does, however, mean you are responsive and regularly present — predictably present. It is very important for instructors to manage their time commitment.

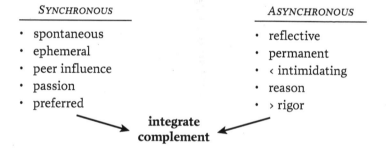

SYNCHRONOUS	ASYNCHRONOUS
• spontaneous	• reflective
• ephemeral	• permanent
• peer influence	• ‹ intimidating
• passion	• reason
• preferred	• › rigor

integrate
complement

FIGURE 2.3. Integrating the strengths of spontaneous verbal and written communication

Organizational design must also consider how to structure the course in terms of blending face-to-face and online learning. This phase of the design process involves thoughtfully integrating synchronous face-to-face and asynchronous online learning experiences. Integrating face-to-face and online communication requires an appreciation of the strengths of spontaneous verbal and reflective written communication (Figure 2.3).

Another organizational issue is matching the content to the mode of delivery. Some material may be best suited to a face-to-face or online context. A risk is that online activities will be viewed as a separate exercise and may not be perceived as having much relevance or importance as to what is happening in the face-to-face class. Online activities must be congruent with anticipated goals in the subsequent face-to-face class. That is, the face-to-face class must build upon the results of the online activities and be congruent with the learning outcomes and assessment procedures for the course (Table 2.2).

TABLE 2.2. Aligning learning outcomes, assessment activities, face-to-face and online learning opportunities, and technology tools

LEARNING OUTCOMES	What do you want your students to know when they have finished your course (e.g., key learning outcomes – knowledge, skills and attitudes)?
ASSESSMENT ACTIVITIES	How will you and your students know if they have achieved these learning outcomes (e.g., opportunities for self-, peer-, and instructor- assessment)?
BEFORE A FACE-TO-FACE SESSION (ONLINE)	How will you help students determine what prior knowledge and experience they have with the assessment activity?
DURING A FACE-TO-FACE SESSION	How will students synchronously interact and engage with the assessment activity?
AFTER A FACE-TO-FACE SESSION (ONLINE)	What portion of this assessment activity will require reflective time for interaction and communication?
TECHNOLOGY TOOLS	What tools could be used to help organize, facilitate, and direct these assessment activities?

In addition, Table 2.3 provides examples of activities that support systematic inquiry, discourse, and reflection.

TABLE 2.3. Examples of activities that support systematic inquiry, discourse, and reflection

ACTIVITY	DESCRIPTION
Student home page	Have the students construct a home page in a learning management system (e.g., Blackboard) where they post a digital image of themselves, a short biography, and their goals for the course. Icebreaker activities and opening discussions can then be designed for the first face-to-face session, which capitalize on the information collected and shared in these student home pages.
Course outline activity	On the first day of class, hand out copies of your course outline and review the key points within a brief Microsoft PowerPoint presentation. Give students 10 to 15 minutes to read the course outline and underline, highlight or make notes about any questions, issues or concerns they have. Next, ask students to form small groups to discuss their questions and try to help each other resolve them. Indicate that you will address questions that remain after they have first attempted to answer them within their small groups. Be sure to allow an appropriate amount of time for students to complete this process. Then ask students how many had questions that were satisfactorily answered in the small group. Remind them that fellow students can often help them see things in a new light, and point out that they should frequently discuss questions with other students. Suggest that they exchange, names, phone numbers, and e-mails with several other students and then use these peers as a first line of support (i.e., share class notes, study for tests, review draft assignments, etc.).
	Note: This entire exercise could also be completed within a learning management system, prior to or during the first week of the course. Post your course outline, create and post a narrated Microsoft PowerPoint presentation (e.g., Adobe Connect) that summarizes the highlights of your outline, and set up small group discussion forums to

facilitate student discussion and resolve course-related questions, issues, or concerns. The instructor can answer questions still remaining during a face-to-face class session or within the main discussion area of your learning management site.

Introductory survey	Prior to the first day of class, send an e-mail to students indicating that you will be using a learning management system (e.g., Blackboard) to support the course and that they are required to log onto the site and complete an introductory survey (perhaps focused on assessing the prior knowledge or experience students have with the course objectives and/or discovering why students are taking the class and what they hope to achieve through the experience). The instructor can then post the survey results to the learning management system and have students discuss the results in small groups on the first class session. Sample introductory survey questions are provided in Appendix 1.

DELIVERY

The second design challenge is to consider the dynamics of delivery. From a cognitive presence perspective, as a discussion develops it will often be necessary to diagnose misconceptions, provide relevant information/insights, and encourage students to reach some form of resolution. This will demand more direct instruction. The process of migrating from facilitation to more direct instruction may repeat itself throughout a course and is especially relevant to bring major assignments to a conclusion.

Based on the second principle, the delivery of a meaningful learning experience is designed by integrating discourse and reflection. This is complicated by the choice between verbal or written communication. Discourse in a synchronous verbal environment has many motivational advantages and, if it is well facilitated, students will achieve the intended goals. However, asynchronous communication has another distinct advantage in terms of critical discourse. Students are able to reflect upon their comments when engaged in an asynchronous online discussion forum. A good example of the differential benefits and applications of synchronous and asynchronous communication is brainstorming. Brainstorming ideas in a face-to-face setting will be energetic, exciting, and productive. However, brainstorming in an online context will generally be more focused and generate fewer but more relevant (i.e., quality) ideas. Online discussions provide opportunities for students who do not feel comfortable participating in spontaneous face-to-face dialogue and debate. Some may still be reluctant participants. While attending to social presence issues may mitigate this, there may be cognitive presence opportunities to engage these students as well. The use of a reflective and rigorous form of communication – the written word – has the potential to encourage a higher quality of interaction for more students. A word of caution: The quality of response may be undermined when grades are assigned based upon frequency of response. While a grade may be assigned for participation, the key to quality interaction is to ensure that the discussion is central to the educational objective and that students meta-cognitively consider the nature of their contribution to the discussion. That is, consider having students label (i.e., script) the nature of their response from the perspective of the inquiry process – that is, an exploratory contribution, an attempt at integration, or perhaps a suggested resolution.

The following techniques will encourage and foster cognitive presence in blended environments:

1. Identify, present, and continually refer back to the key concepts you want students to take away from the course.

2. Make explicit the knowledge, skills, and attitudes students should learn and develop through course activities.

3. Use triangulation to provide multiple representations and multiple activities to reach the stated objectives.

4. Engage in provocative, open-ended Socratic questioning with a view toward encouraging experimentation,

supporting divergent thinking and many perspectives, particularly in ongoing online discussion.

5. Promote active engagement in practical applications of knowledge and shared summaries of discussion.

As noted previously, online activities must be well integrated into the face-to-face activities, and vice-versa. Face-to-face time must be valued and not wasted by only delivering content. This time is best used for engagement and higher order learning. For example, complex concepts are best explored in a face-to-face context; however, this does not prohibit having the students read content and begin an online discussion to identify areas of confusion before the face-to-face class. Moreover, consideration must be given to follow-up activities. If further reflection and discussion is beneficial, then this can be sustained in a reflective online environment. Some topics such as an assigned reading may be successfully handled fully online with students providing a summary followed by critiques from other students.

ASSESSMENT

Assessment structures reveal what is valued and shape how students approach their learning. Assessment must be consistent with deep and meaningful learning. If students are assessed by recall of factual material and a heavy workload, they will resist approaches that encourage critical discourse and reflection. They will expect the instructor to simply present the content in a timely and clearly structured manner. It is interesting to note that deep approaches to learning are associated, not only with appropriate assessment, but with teaching presence in the form of facilitation and choice, regardless of delivery method (Entwistle & Tait, 1990). Assessment very much shapes the quality of learning and the quality of teaching. In short, students do what is rewarded. For this reason one must be sure to reward activities that encourage deep and meaningful approaches to learning.

Qualitative feedback can be effectively provided in a face-to-face or online context. Online discussion boards are one mechanism. However, quantitative formative assessment online has an efficiency advantage. For example, formative online quizzes can provide feedback when needed by the student and do not need intervention or grading by the instructor. Online quizzes can be used for student use only or recorded for grades.

Summative assessment is about assessing competence. Summative assessment makes a judgment, based on quantitative and qualitative data, about achievement related to intended learning outcomes. If the intended learning outcomes are deep and meaningful learning, then assessment must be based on assignments that encourage critical thinking and inquiry. Such assignments can be analyses of case studies, article reviews, and individual or collaborative projects. Grading a collaborative assignment needs special consideration as tensions and inequities may arise in terms of individual contributions. For this reason, consideration should be given to having students work collaboratively to a point, but then have students submit individual assignments based on different perspectives or components of a larger problem. Even though students submit individual assignments, the group may, for example, do a collaborative presentation with a grade assigned for the group.

Self-assessment must be used with caution. While self-assessment may contribute to motivation and satisfaction, the association with learning is moderate (Sitzman et al., 2010). Therefore, to use it for summative assessment would carry validity concerns. With these caveats, the purposes for using self-assessment need to be very carefully understood. To use it for formative feedback may be advantageous. In this regard, it could be used to encourage metacognitive awareness by assessing one's responses.

Student evaluations or ratings of instruction can also be used to evaluate the effectiveness of the blended course design. This evaluation would consider content, teaching and learning experiences, student assessment methods, and, most significantly, the appropriate use of face-to-face and online learning modes of delivery. Common strengths of blended designs are the rigorous design structure and a permanent record for systematic review and upgrading. This opportunity for improvement can enhance the course and provide evidence of effectiveness and may also serve as a model to others when designing their own blended learning courses.

When evaluating a blended learning design, there are tools that can help us gather important data. One useful tool is the Community of Inquiry (CoI) Survey (Arbaugh et al., 2008). The CoI Survey is based on the CoI framework and can measure perceived social, cognitive, and teaching presence. Together, these measures will provide an assessment of the community of inquiry and identify areas where the course has been successful or may need to be redesigned. As we have stated previously, the strength of blended learning is providing for active, engaged, and collaborative learning. For this reason, another tool that may be used to assess engagement is the Classroom Survey of Student Engagement (CLASSE). This tool is the course-based derivative of the National Survey of Student Engagement (NSSE), and it focuses on student perceptions regarding the amount of active and collaborative learning, interactions with faculty members, and level of academic challenge in a specific course (Ouimet & Smallwood, 2005).

CONCLUSION

The time and attention given to its design are distinct features of a blended learning course. The practical reality is that a blended learning course design brings many challenges and decisions; time must be given on the front end if we are to integrate the differential strengths of face-to-face and online communication thoughtfully. Given the inherent complexities in a blended learning design, it is wise to keep things as simple as possible. That means limiting content, methods, and technology, while ensuring that intended educational goals are met. The previous discussion was intended to provide strategies and identify issues with regard to the organization of content objectives, the delivery of instruction, and the evaluation of learning outcomes — all of which need to be matched with face-to-face and online communication characteristics and possibilities.

3 Facilitation

You can teach a student a lesson for a day; but if you can teach him
to learn by creating curiosity, he will continue the learning process as
long as he lives. (Bedford cited in Geerdink, 2013, n.p.)

INTRODUCTION

The existence of this book is testimony to the interest in, and value
of, blended learning environments. Of particular interest is the role
that faculty play. This role is key to a successful blended learning
environment, and a particular requirement called *facilitation of
learning* is an essential piece. In contrast, blended learning experiences created by adding online access to course documentation and
content material, without instructor presence and interaction, are
blends of content but not learning experiences. Instructors must
learn and employ the skills "to teach and learn in increasingly net-
worked, technology-rich, digital (and face-to-face) classrooms"

(Clifford, Friesen, & Lock, 2004, p. 19); virtual classrooms become the teaching and learning spaces in blended learning.

According to Bonk, Kim, and Zeng (2004), "Blended learning is typically more complicated and multifaceted than either fully online or face-to-face learning ... instructors must know when to shift gears or add new tasks or resources and when to let the learners wander off and explore their own interests" (p. 17). This speaks to the piece of blended teaching that is facilitation—arranging and supporting learner activities and learning, in both online and face-to-face classrooms. Facilitation exists as the central activity of teaching in an educational community of inquiry that emerges from the activity between students and instructor. Facilitative actions, on the part of both the students and the instructor, create the climate, support discourse, and monitor learning such that presence can emerge and inquiry occurs. In the act of facilitation learners connect to each other and the instructor, engage with the content, are cognitively present as intellectual agents, and carry out all actions central to the development and maintenance of the learning community.

This chapter revisits the notions of teaching presence, its central elements, and how facilitation aligns with other elements of teaching presence in blended learning environments. This allows detailed consideration of the facilitation of social and cognitive presence and the principles that guide blended facilitation. Of all aspects of the Community of Inquiry framework, the activities of facilitation are the most critical; facilitation manages the overlaps between all three presences and is at the core of the dynamics of a community of inquiry.

TEACHING PRESENCE REVISITED

Teaching presence is explained as the effort and activity around the design, facilitation, and direction of cognitive and social processes in learning communities created to foster inquiry, for the purpose of realizing personally meaningful and educationally worthwhile learning. It is the central element around which other activities in a community of inquiry manoeuvre. The three elements of teaching presence—design and organization, facilitation, and direct instruction—are distinct but not mutually exclusive. *Design and organization* must include activity appropriate to the facilitation of a community, a constructed learning environment, and the engagement of students and teachers and learners. *Facilitation* is the facet of teaching presence that ensures that social presence is established among community members and, in turn, that cognitive processes are directed to personally meaningful and educationally worthwhile outcomes. Facilitation remains distinct from direct instruction in that too much domination on the part of the instructor will intimidate learners and diminish engagement. *Direct instruction*, however, provides necessary leadership for content accuracy and boundaries. Facilitation, much richer in nuance and engagement, is the action of choice for as long as the learners are reaching the learning outcomes.

Facilitation is described as the necessary support and guidance provided for learners. While chiefly required for the facilitation of reflection and discourse, facilitation in a blended community of inquiry becomes multitudinously complex. First, it requires that all the necessary components outlined for facilitation of an online community of inquiry (Garrison, Anderson, & Archer, 2001) be appropriately created face-to-face. Second, it requires that the key overlaps between the necessary presences of a community of inquiry—setting climate, supporting discourse, and monitoring and regulating learning—be appropriately facilitated both face-to-face and online. And third, through facilitation the online community of inquiry will be experienced as linked and contiguous with the face-to-face community; while they can emerge separately, in a blended learning environment they must converge as one.

It is important to note that the term *teaching presence* refers to the action and role of teaching, and not uniquely to the instructor of record. Facilitators must acknowledge and support the role of teacher among students, when appropriate. Students in a community of inquiry are engaged in a way that fosters self-regulation and monitoring, of themselves and fellow learners. It is for this reason that we refer to this element as *teaching* presence and not *teacher* presence. In other words, everyone has the opportunity to contribute by way of facilitation and direct instruction. In a blended environment, the faculty member, as facilitator, must provide the opportunity and allow similarly for such peer interaction and teaching face-to-face as well as online. The challenge, of course, is allowing for such activity while staying connected enough to redirect any inappropriate actions on the part of any particular student. This issue can be pre-empted with action to set an appropriate, respectful climate at the beginning of the course.

PRINCIPLES OF FACILITATION

The combination or blending of online and face-to-face interactions results in a new learning environment that necessitates significant role adjustments for instructors; there is a need to understand the concept of teaching presence for deep and meaningful learning outcomes. While we present this as something necessary for blended learning environments, it is, in fact, an imperative for education in a new society (Cleveland-Innes & Garrison, 2011; Keller, 2008). The following principles of facilitation for social and cognitive presence in a blended learning environment are part of this required change.

SOCIAL PRESENCE

For students to be socially present they must have the opportunity to interact. The importance of social and academic interaction in the experience of students, first socially, and the impact on deep learning through cognitive presence, is well established (Cleveland-Innes & Emes, 2005).

PRINCIPLE: *Establish community and cohesion.*

A community of inquiry emerges and maintains itself through the purposeful engagement, interaction, and relationships between members of the group. The facilitator begins the work of each community by encouraging, modeling, and supporting these activities, such that each member of the group may become familiar with, and possibly find a link to, other members of the group. The strength and tenor of these links becomes a measure of the amount of cohesion found within each group; this determines whether the group becomes a community or not. The more developmental and meaningful the engagement and interaction, the stronger the links, the greater the cohesion, and, once community is established, the more likely deep and meaningful learning will occur. In the initial meeting of a group of students, the facilitator plays a key role in ensuring that community develops. In a blended environment, this requires modeling and encouraging such activity both face-to-face and online.

It would be a significant error to assume that social presence does not have to be fostered and managed face-to-face. In reality, it may more difficult and fraught with more challenges than being socially present online. This is particularly true in large classes; hence the benefit of blending online interaction in support of the community that also meets face-to-face.

Social presence requires that one present oneself, socially and emotionally, in honest and valid ways. In front of the classroom, instructors present varying demeanours, across time and people. In the all-important overlap between teaching presence and social presence, setting climate occurs. First, in the hands of the role of the teacher, this requires that the instructor set the tone of openness, fairness, safety, and debate. Development of such a climate and community can be fostered in both the face-to-face and online learning environments of a blended course or program. Table 3.1 presents a series of strategies for facilitating social presence in the face-to-face and online components.

TABLE 3.1. Facilitating social presence face-to-face and online

STRATEGY	FACE-TO FACE	ONLINE
Provide opportunities for initial introductions and ongoing social interaction.	As indicated previously, this may appear challenging where student numbers are large. First, acknowledge to the class that interaction is important and will be particularly fostered online. Second, provide the opportunity for small group interaction in at least the first few classes, continuously if possible. The less "talking head" (transmission by the instructor) the higher the engagement.	Ask for and create the appropriate virtual space for introductions, including text and photos, audio, and/or video clips. Be explicit about the need to get to know each other, to encourage social interaction online (but separate from academic discussion).
Set agreed-upon, shared norms for operating together in the learning community.	This is best done in the first class, after some one-to-one interaction among students has occurred. Ask students to reflect for a moment on their most valuable and satisfying classroom experiences, and consider what informal rules or norms were at work in this setting. Ask for suggestions and document them. Process for the following types of group norms:	Ensure students understand norms set face-to-face apply online, but clarify any unique implementation. How many, and what type of, posts characterize being there. How much is too much? Post agreed-upon norms, with clarification, in the virtual classroom. Remind students of the norms when necessary.

	1. Everyone shows up. 2. Everyone participates. 3. Start on time. 4. Respect the airtime. 5. Respect individual perspectives. 6. Agree to disagree. 7. No hurtful, hateful comments about individuals or groups. Once documented, ask if anyone has significant concerns about any of the norms. Process and reword as necessary. Tell the students the same norms apply online, and the list will be posted in the virtual classroom. Remind students of the norms for each class early in the term; provide reminders when necessary.	
Discuss the unique nature of each learning mode and the blending of such.	Be explicit about the similarities and differences between the face-to-face and virtual environments. Be clear about expectation regarding presence in both. Outline any marks assigned to presence or participation, where appropriate. Process for any questions or concerns.	Post about, and discuss online, the similarities and differences between the face-to-face and virtual environments. Reiterate expectations regarding presence in both. Post online any marks assigned to presence or participation, where appropriate.

STRATEGY	FACE-TO FACE	ONLINE
Outline required activities and arrange support for students concerned about role requirements.	Document questions and concerns. Students experience significant role adjustment when learning online, which will be no less significant when working in a blended environment. Discussing these possible issues face-to-face, ahead of significant engagement online, may waylay such concerns and increase adjustment and comfort working online. Data suggests that online students are challenged by the new role identity of learner, the use of the learning technology, the design of new learning activities such as text-based discussions, the increased level of interaction, and the role of online instructor (Cleveland-Innes, Garrison & Kinsel, 2008).	Discuss the possibility that students may experience significant role adjustment when learning online. Provide opportunity for students to state any concerns about the online environment —or anything related to the course. Create a FAQ (frequently asked questions) area online to present information about the technology and working online.
Discuss the unique nature of each learning mode and the blending of such.	Traditionally, social interaction is frowned upon in face-to-face classrooms (no whispering or passing notes in class!). Online environments provide the opportunity to allow for social interaction separate from the content-based, academic discussions.	Separate discussions areas that relate strictly to social discussions and community development, and forums related to the content and key questions related to the material and learning objectives. Early in the course, be explicit about these expectations.

STRATEGY	FACE-TO FACE	ONLINE
	Provide opportunities for students to introduce themselves face-to-face if possible. Emphasize that social interaction will be allowed, even encouraged, in appropriate areas or discussion boards online. As community develops, students will use pre-class and post-class time to greet and converse with each other.	
Provide explicit directions for all course activities; outline and discuss course content, skill and activity goals, and expectations.	Use early classes' face-to-face time to outline and answer questions about activities, readings, assignments, and schedules. Create an explicit syllabus with detailed outcomes, expectations, assignments, and timelines. This document can be handed out in paper and posted online.	Post questions and answers online that emerged face-to-face about activities, readings, assignments, and schedules. Post the explicit syllabus with detailed outcomes, expectations, assignments, and timelines.
Be clear about learner choice and flexibility.	Where possible, provide learner choice in activity, assignments, content, and leadership. Be clear about these opportunities in the first class.	Be clear about online learner choice in activity, assignments, content, and leadership. For example, provide opportunities to facilitate discussion, post questions of interest and interesting and valuable resources related to the course subject.

STRATEGY	FACE-TO FACE	ONLINE
Provide activities for instructors and students to share experiences and support one another.	Arrange opportunities for instructor-student interaction—one-on-one and group based—for social and academic interaction. Interaction between student and instructor fosters trust and reduces barriers to learning. Be present socially, as a real and affective person. As community develops over time, social interaction will fold into academic discourse (Akyol, Vaughan & Garrison, 2011).	Use synchronous and asynchronous tools to support instructor-student interaction – one-on-one and group based – for social and academic interaction. Arrange virtual office hours for synchronous chat. Ensure students know how to use these tools. Be present online socially, as a real and affective person.

COGNITIVE PRESENCE

Facilitating social interaction fosters engagement and a sense of trust, safety, and familiarity such that social presence may emerge; this is central to setting the climate for rigorous debate and discourse and collaborative activity. Pushing beyond social interaction to academic interaction and critical discourse moves the community from social presence to cognitive presence and into deep and meaningful learning.

PRINCIPLE: *Establish inquiry dynamics (purposeful inquiry).*

The inquiry process is both embedded in, and an outcome of, a cohesive community of learners. The inquiry dynamics are the engagement and interaction at multiple levels of complexity and meaning. The practical inquiry process, fundamental to cognitive presence, requires increasing amounts of cognitive effort and complexity. This process of changing complexity must be facilitated through appropriate discourse—from triggering event, exploration, and integration, to resolution. Facilitation is most critical in the earliest stages of interaction; direct instruction becomes more important as complexity increases. In other words, facilitation is necessary to set in motion the inquiry dynamics, but direct instruction may be employed where facilitation of discourse no longer moves the inquiry to integration and resolution.

The opportunity for increased interaction, timely reflection, and continuous debate online provides a very supportive environment for inquiry dynamics. The following indicators of facilitation can be used to support inquiry face-to-face and online:

1. Maintain a comfortable climate for learning.
2. Focus the discussion on specific issues.
3. Identify areas of agreement/disagreement.
4. Seek to reach consensus/understanding.
5. Encourage, acknowledge, and reinforce contributions.
6. Draw in participants, prompting discussion.
7. Assess and make explicit the efficacy of the process.
8. Refer to resources, e.g., textbook, articles, Internet, personal experiences.
9. Summarize the discussion.

These strategies, and others, can be used to support required facilitation of cognitive presence. Table 3.2 presents strategies for the face-to-face and online component.

TABLE 3.2. Facilitating cognitive presence face-to-face and online

STRATEGY	FACE-TO FACE	ONLINE
Facilitation is based on collaboration and discourse; use collaborative learning	Inquiry dynamics are supported through questions that trigger use of subject matter.	Discourse refers to the dialogic interaction characterizing online discussion. To make

STRATEGY	FACE-TO FACE	ONLINE
principles in small group discussion and joint projects.	Triggering events must be preceded by attention to the required content for considering answers to the question or curious attention to the material. The instructor can bring readings, and other self-regulated student activity, to life by bringing attention to key points. This can be done with visuals, stories, questions, problems, and presentation of information. Collaboration of learning activity can include instructor to large group (e.g., asking questions, showing visuals for analysis, showing video clips for discussion). It can also include group work, with groups that include or exclude instructor input. Collaborative learning can extend beyond triggers to exploration and integration, and eventually to resolution (e.g., what will/might/ should occur?).	discourse collaborative requires that the instructor move out of the role of expert and into the role of process leader and learning support. Link student comments to the content, to examples, and to each other. Create small groups of discussion and the opportunity for joint projects in assignments and activities.
Model and encourage responsiveness and immediacy behaviours in interactions with students.	Show up early and ready to lead the class. Be responsive to students with eye contact, nods, smiles, and interaction. Attend to any queries	Be regularly present online without taking over the discussion. Rather than respond to each individual post, provide synthesis and encouragement.

STRATEGY	FACE-TO FACE	ONLINE
	or concerns right away, even if it is just to make a date to explore the question or issue further.	
Model and encourage affective expression by sharing experiences and beliefs in discussions.	Recent findings indicate the presence of emotion in education environments, particularly in relation to achievement motivation and engagement. Affective expression is acceptable and possibly beneficial, in appropriate amounts.	Be real and affective, rather than cool, calculating, and objective. The online environment requires accommodation for the lack of non-verbal cues that transmit information about tenor and emotion. Share your thoughts, feelings and experiences — where appropriate to the context and content.
Share the facilitation of discourse by having students summarize discussions.	Enhance the possibility of cognitive engagement by allowing students to lead discussions and/or present content. Share the lead in class.	This is somewhat trickier online; if students are off the mark in their summations, it is in text and semi-permanent. Monitor and make corrections with care.
Model and encourage critical questioning, divergent thinking, and multiple perspectives in discussion through provocative, open-ended questions.	Ask reflective and critical questions during class: So, what does this mean? What's missing in this? What else might be influencing this?	Online, you can also ask reflective and critical questions. Here the link to the material becomes somewhat more important as students can't ask for clarification and get an immediate response. Open-ended, abstract questions can be augmented with clear reference to content or examples.

STRATEGY	FACE-TO FACE	ONLINE
Model and request practical applications of knowledge and/or formulate and resolve a problem in small group discussions.	Using a problem-based approach, provide opportunities to explore, apply, and integrate subject matter content to well-known, meaningful issues – in small, medium, and large group activities.	The above supports this strategy as well. Use questions that go beyond the immediate factual knowledge into practical application. Text can get tedious here; use audio or video inserts wherever possible. Facilitate to resolution – what do the students think could or should be done?
Encourage and support the progression of inquiry in discussion and small group activities through triggering events, exploration, and integration to resolution.	Make the cognitive progression explicit. Assist students through layered activities that build on each other through triggering events, exploration, and integration, to resolution. Teach committed relativism; have students take a position and defend it, knowing that there are multiple perspectives and layers of authoritative knowledge (Perry, 1981).	Again, make the cognitive progression explicit. Layer the discussion so it builds through triggering events, exploration, and integration, to resolution. Reemphasize committed relativism; have students take a position and defend it, knowing that there are multiple perspectives (Perry, 1981).
Use development or scaffolding of both content and processes to support behaviours that move discourse through integration to resolution.	Use questions, debate, quotations, and evidence in varying degrees to demonstrate to students multiple strategies of argument.	Along with Perry's notions of committed relativism are important tenets of argumentation. Post questions and encourage debate with sound evidence in varying degrees to demonstrate to students multiple strategies of argument.

STRATEGY	FACE-TO FACE	ONLINE
Use discussion summaries to identify steps in the knowledge creation process.	Reflect back to students their important points about process and content — what worked, what needs work.	This is easier to do online! However, summaries must be inclusive (try to find something from posts by each student) and corrections carefully made.
Use discussion material to illuminate course content and encourage students to incorporate content from discussions in their assignments.	Identify the link back to course content; use course material with additional support from student experiences and additional resources.	Discussion forums become course content, when accurate and academic. Make sure students recognize and use valuable forums in their learning activities and assignments.
Use peer review to engage students in a cycle of practical inquiry.	Once the practical inquiry cycle is understood and is in use, allow students to provide this same level of feedback to each other. Observe and support. Maximize collaborative activities, such as problem-solving tasks, projects, and small-group discussions. Over time, reduce instructor presence in discussion and increasingly facilitate student-led academic discourse.	This is also a little trickier online. Review norms of operation so peer review is done with respect and support. Provide opportunity for students to facilitate their own forums. Maximize collaborative activities — problem-solving tasks, projects, and small-group discussion.
Maximize virtual connection and collaboration by including synchronous communications; chat, collaborative		Text can get very dry! Use the technology to augment interaction but ensure students are competent or adjusting — don't assume all can

STRATEGY	FACE-TO FACE	ONLINE
whiteboards, interactive video, blogs, wikis, YouTube, Flickr, MySpace, etc.		use, or are comfortable using, any technology tools.

FACILITATING THE BLEND

The face-to-face learning environment has long been dominated by a lecture format, with students passively listening and instructors presenting. This has been criticized as an ineffective way to facilitate learning, and many strategies have been suggested to change this. The opportunity for interaction, discussion, and debate in the online environment has provided more evidence of the value of such activities.

Discussion is not left for the online environment. The notion of blending learning environments through the combination of learning activities face-to-face and virtually is discussed in other places in this book. This review of facilitation in blended environments considers that equal weight, with differing actions, be given to both face-to-face and virtual environments. We share two key critical strategies: make explicit links from activities in one mode to the other, and, where possible, use audio/video clips of face-to-face activity to link to activity online. In other words, make reference in the face-to-face environment current and key activities occurring online, and vice-versa. This mends any seam that may occur between two environments, making the community seamless.

It may be difficult to think of blended facilitation as performing the same action in each environment. In fact, this may not be possible, or desired. However, the desired outcomes related to creating social presence and cognitive presence must be considered as necessary in each environment. In other words, we cannot expect that learners who socially and cognitively present online will also do so when meeting face-to-face. The opposite is also true. This means that, while the instructional activity may or may not be the same, facilitation of each presence must be attended to in each environment, and in the notion of the blend. While it is not necessary to do the same thing in each environment – in fact, this may be difficult – doing some of the same in each environment with explicit reference to the activities at other times and in the other format provides continuity.

It may be that we know more about how to create social and cognitive presence online than face-to-face. This is because of the opportunity for time-independent interaction; learners and the instructor can offer ideas and considerations when, and for as long as, they like. Facilitation strategies that can be variously employed face-to-face or online have been described in this chapter.

CONCLUSION

Collaborative communities emerge, and are sustained, through shared purpose, joint activity, and interaction. These commonalities must be identified, illuminated, and fostered through the leadership of the teacher to facilitate these aspects of community. It is through facilitation that social presence emerges and cognitive presence evolves.

4 Direct Instruction

Direct instruction recognizes the continuous need for the expertise of an experienced and responsible teacher who can identify the ideas and concepts worthy of study, provide the conceptual order, organize learning activities, guide the discourse, offer additional sources of information, diagnose misconceptions, and interject when required.
(Garrison, 2011, p. 60)

INTRODUCTION

At the outset, let's be clear about what direct instruction is not. Direct instruction is not lecturing. While it may provide information, suggestions, and direction, it is not antithetical to collaborative constructive (i.e., engaged) approaches to learning. Direct instruction is about ensuring that students achieve intended learning outcomes in a timely fashion without unnecessary frustration. It is an essential ingredient in any formal educational experience if we are to have assurance that worthwhile learning outcomes are realized.

Direct instruction is a crucial and developmental component of teaching presence in a community of inquiry. It has been shown that students expect structure and leadership (Garrison & Cleveland-Innes, 2005). Moreover, the complexity of blended learning design possibilities necessitates the need for structure and scholarly leadership. Given organizational structure (i.e., instructional design), direct instruction provides the leadership that will focus discourse and resolve issues in ways that facilitation alone is not intended to do. In formal educational learning environments, it is expected that discourse be purposeful, rigorous, and productive. This is the function of direct instruction. Evidence strongly suggests that perceived learning and satisfaction are associated with strong leadership (Akyol & Garrison, 2011b; Garrison, 2011).

Teaching presence has a natural developmental process. As we have explored in previous chapters, design and facilitation responsibilities most often demand the greatest attention as we create communities of inquiry. However, direct instruction issues will inevitably arise in our attempt to sustain open communication, group cohesion, and focused inquiry. These tasks go directly to sustaining a constructive social presence that is the foundation of a community of inquiry. From a social presence perspective, direct instruction is intended to maintain the educational and academic climate and direction.

Direct instruction, however, is also about focusing and resolving cognitive presence issues. Direct instruction recognizes the continuous need for "the expertise of an experienced and responsible teacher who can identify the ideas and concepts worthy of study, provide the conceptual order, organize learning activities, guide the discourse, offer additional sources of information, diagnose misconceptions, and interject when required" (Garrison, 2011, p. 60). Through these direct interventions we can be assured of an effective and efficient educational experience. That said, it is not inevitable that the instructor of record provide these services.

Notwithstanding the essential role of an experienced instructor, participants in a community of inquiry must be encouraged and afforded the opportunity to provide direction when necessary. The instructor should intervene only when significant issues arise that arrest the progress of timely development. These interventions must be limited if participants are to gain metacognitive awareness, responsibility, and control (monitoring and management) of their learning. Nothing will shut down discourse and undermine group cohesion faster than excessive direct intervention by the instructor. This goes to the core of understanding that teaching presence is a distributed responsibility and realizing that the ultimate goal of learning is to think and learn.

In previous chapters, we have explored the practical implications of the teaching presence principles for the design and facilitation of a blended community of inquiry. We now focus our attention on the direct instruction principles for creating and sustaining a blended community of inquiry. A successful blended community of inquiry and learning experience will be shaped by more than passive guidance. It will require content and pedagogical expertise to anticipate and proactively shape the environment and direction of the educational process in real time.

SOCIAL PRESENCE

The first principle for direct instruction is associated with sustaining a supportive environment and addressing issues that may undermine the trust and sense of belonging within the group.

PRINCIPLE: *Sustain respect and responsibility.*

This principle is associated with social presence responsibilities. We need to remind ourselves that social presence is concerned with open communication, group cohesion, and interpersonal relationships. Maintaining an open and cohesive community of inquiry requires a sensitive and sustained focus. Sustaining the climate, committing to the collaborative process, and developing interpersonal relationships is the essence of this principle. During the facilitation process, the challenge was to establish these properties of a community of inquiry. Once established, the challenge is to ensure that they grow and to address issues that may undermine the climate that mediates academic discourse.

From a social presence perspective, one of the important responsibilities of direct instruction is to be active in ensuring that open communication is not undermined by insensitive personal comments or overly critical, unproductive postings. Participants must be encouraged to question the substance of messages, but this must be done respectfully, constructively, and with academic insight. Communication and trust is a particular challenge in online environments, and particular attention is required to ensure that the community and working groups maintain a collegial atmosphere if they are to stay collaboratively focused on the task. That is, they remain trustful and identify with the group (maintain goal clarity and group cohesion) to ensure successful completion of collaborative tasks.

Group cohesion is also enhanced through interpersonal relationships. If issues are addressed when they arise, then participants will naturally stay connected and develop interpersonal relationships that will support learning during and beyond the course of studies. Particular attention needs to be given to these issues when working asynchronously online. Resolving relationship conflict is more challenging in virtual contexts (Bierly, Stark, & Kessler, 2009), and direct instructional interventions will be required to ensure effective collaboration. On the other hand, much can be done in the face-to-face environment to mitigate social presence issues that may arise over time. Relationship conflict can be mitigated in face-to-face settings.

Engagement is central to a blended learning experience. The strength of blended learning is the ability to create and sustain engagement in a community of inquiry. Direct instruction must be seen as enhancing academic engagement. At the outset we need to note that sustaining productive discourse and cognitive presence requires the right balance of social presence. Too much social presence can undermine inquiry as much as too little. It is crucial that direct instruction ensures that personal relationships do not inhibit students from challenging ideas and offering constructive alternatives. One thing to watch for is personal/social relationships getting in the way of students providing honest critiques of each other's work. This may be a particular issue in a face-to-face environment. The converse may be a more likely challenge in a virtual environment.

The opportunity for greater independence and reflection in a virtual environment is an advantage but also a challenge. This raises the importance of direct instruction if we are to ensure open communication (climate/trust), cohesion (focus/collaboration), and the development of positive interpersonal relationships (familiarity with abilities/beliefs). Direct instruction addresses the strengths and weaknesses of face-to-face and online learning dynamics. All of this is directed to resolving problems and enhancing learning outcomes.

Guidelines associated with this principle are to be supportive, but expect students to be self-directed and work collaboratively to complete tasks. From a teaching presence perspective, there will be a stage in terms of group dynamics where tensions and conflicts will arise. It is crucial that the teacher addresses these situations directly and resolves conflicts, by negotiating expectations or correcting a student who is out of line (e.g., using excessive or flaming messages). Students should also feel that they can question the teacher and will be treated respectfully. Team-building activities will give students the opportunity to develop connections and build community support to accomplish the assigned tasks.

Effective educational strategies for this first principle of direct instruction include providing students with opportunities to discuss and clarify expectations, roles and responsibilities of team members through the use of inquiry-based project work guidelines, learning contracts, and assessment activities.

Inquiry-based project work involves a group of students investigating a worthy question, issue, problem, or idea. This is the type of authentic project work that those working in the disciplines actually undertake to create or build knowledge. These projects involve serious engagement and investigation. Two resources that we have found of particular value to guide inquiry-based project work are the *Team-Based Learning Collaborative* and the *Galileo Educational Network.*[1]

Team-based learning (TBL) involves sequencing individual tasks, group work, and immediate feedback to create an educational environment in which students increasingly hold each other accountable for each other's learning and academic success. The Galileo Educational Network has developed an inquiry-based project rubric that consists of eight dimensions. The key components and descriptors for this rubric are highlighted in Table 4.1.

TABLE 4.1. Inquiry-based project rubric

DIMENSION OF INQUIRY	DESCRIPTORS
1. Authenticity	• The inquiry study emanates from a question, problem, or exploration that has meaning to the students.
	• The inquiry study originates with an issue, problem, question, exploration, or topic that provides opportunities to create or produce something that contributes to the world's knowledge.

---

1   These resources are available online: *Team-Based Learning Collaborative* (http://www.teambasedlearning.org/) and the *Galileo Educational Network* (http://www.galileo.org/inquiry-what.html).

DIMENSION OF INQUIRY	DESCRIPTORS
	• The tasks or task require(s) a variety of roles or perspectives.
2. Academic rigour	• The inquiry study leads students to build knowledge that leads to deep understanding.
	• Students are provided with multiple, flexible ways to approach the problem, issue, or question under study that use methods of inquiry central to the disciplines that underpin the problem, issue, or question.
	• The inquiry study encourages students to develop habits of mind that encourage them to ask questions concerning the following:
	› evidence (How do we know what we know?)
	› viewpoint (Who is speaking?)
	› pattern and connection (What causes what?)
	› supposition (How might things have been different?)
	› why it matters (Who cares?)
3. Assessment	• On-going assessment is woven into the design of the inquiry study providing timely descriptive feedback and utilizing a range of methods, including peer and self-assessment. Assessment guides student learning and teacher's instructional planning.
	• The study provides opportunities for students to reflect on their learning using clear criteria that they helped to set. The students use these reflections to set learning goals, establish next steps, and develop effective learning strategies.
	• Teachers, peers, experts from outside the classroom, and the student are involved in the assessment of the work.
4. Beyond the school	• The study requires students to address a semi-structured question, issue, or problem that is relevant to curriculum outcomes, but grounded in life and work beyond the school.
	• The study requires students to develop organizational and self-management skills in order to complete the study.

DIMENSION OF INQUIRY	DESCRIPTORS
	• The study leads students to acquire and use competencies expected in high-performance work organizations (e.g., team work, problem solving, communications, decision making, and project management).
5. Use of digital technologies	• Technology is used in a purposeful manner that demonstrates an appreciation of new ways of thinking and doing. The technology is essential in accomplishing the task.
	• The study requires students to determine which technologies are most appropriate to the task.
	• The study requires students to conduct research, share information, make decisions, solve problems, create meaning, and communicate with various audiences inside and outside the classroom.
	• The study makes excellent use of digital resources.
	• The study requires sophisticated use of multimedia/ hypermedia software, video, conferencing, simulation, databases, programming, etc.
6. Active exploration	• The study requires students to spend significant amounts of time doing fieldwork, design work, labs, interviews, studio work, construction, etc.
	• The study requires students to engage in real, authentic investigations using a variety of media, methods, and sources.
	• The study requires students to communicate what they are learning with a variety of audiences through presentations, exhibitions, websites, wikis, blogs, etc.
7. Connecting with experts	• The study requires students to observe and interact with experts with relevant expertise and experience in a variety of situations.

Dimension of Inquiry	Descriptors
	• The tasks are designed in collaboration with experts, either directly or indirectly. The inquiry requires adults to collaborate with one another and with students on the design and assessment of the inquiry work.
8. Elaborated communication	• Students have extended opportunities to support, challenge, and respond to each other's ideas as they negotiate a collective understanding of relevant concepts.
	• Students have opportunities to negotiate the flow of conversation within small and large group discussions.
	• Students have opportunities to choose forms of expression to express their understanding.
	• The inquiry provides opportunities for students to communicate what they are learning with a variety of audiences.

Adapted from Galileo Educational Network (2011)

In addition, learning contracts can be a useful tool for helping students to plan and complete inquiry-based project work. These contracts should be constructed by the student and reviewed by the instructor for constructive feedback and suggestions for modification. Both the student and the instructor should sign the final version of the learning contract. The contract then serves as an outline for the project and a tool to aid in the assessment process. Modification of the learning contract may become necessary as the learning experience progresses. Modified contracts should be approved and signed by both students and the instructor. Table 4.2 is an example of a learning contract, adapted from the work of Knowles (1986).

TABLE 4.2. Sample learning contract

WHAT ARE YOU GOING TO LEARN? (OBJECTIVES)	HOW ARE YOU GOING TO LEARN IT? (RESOURCES AND STRATEGIES)	TARGET DATE FOR COMPLETION	HOW ARE YOU GOING TO KNOW THAT YOU LEARNED IT? (EVIDENCE)	HOW ARE YOU GOING TO PROVE THAT YOU LEARNED IT? (VERIFICATION)	INSTRUCTOR FEEDBACK (ASSESSMENT
Itemize what you want to be able to do or know when completed.	What do you have to do in order meet each of the objectives defined?	When do you plan to complete each task?	What is the specific task that you are to complete in order to demonstrate learning?	Who will receive the product of your learning and how will they assess it?	How well was the task completed? Provide an assessment decision.

I have reviewed and find acceptable the above learning contract.

Date: Student: Instructor:

Adapted from Knowles (1986)

For an inquiry-based project or activity, it is critical that the assessment techniques are congruent and clearly aligned with the learning outcomes for the course. As demonstrated in the Galileo inquiry rubric (http://www.galileo.org/research/publications/rubric.pdf), an instructor should provide a range of methods and opportunities for student assessment. Chapter 5 will provide specific examples of self-, peer-, and instructor-assessment strategies.

COGNITIVE PRESENCE

The second direct instruction principle addresses cognitive presence issues. This concerns scholarly leadership and is associated with critical discourse, reflection, and progression through the phases of practical inquiry.

PRINCIPLE: *Sustain inquiry that moves to resolution*

Direct instruction is specifically tasked with ensuring systematic and disciplined inquiry. Sustaining purposeful inquiry includes several overlapping responsibilities. The overriding responsibility of direct instruction is to ensure that participants move through the inquiry phases and that they do so in a timely manner. This was one of the challenges revealed in the early research into the Community of Inquiry framework (Garrison, 2011). In addition to task design deficiencies, it was found that direct instruction was lacking in terms of moving to resolution. Ensuring progression to the resolution phase in the context of collaborative inquiry requires that participants maintain focus on the task and that issues are resolved quickly. While focus and progression are important issues, this should not exclude exploring worthwhile unintended avenues of inquiry. This must, however, be managed in the context of insuring that intended educational goals are achieved.

To ensure developmental progression requires persistent attention to a number of related issues such as diagnosing misconceptions, providing essential content, and offering conceptual order when necessary. At times it may be necessary to renegotiate expectations. Similarly, intervening to address misconceptions and unproductive lines of inquiry in a collaborative and non-authoritarian manner is essential to maintaining participation and cohesion in a community of inquiry. While it is advantageous that participants take on this responsibility, as much as can be expected (remaining true to the essence of the teaching presence construct), inevitably the content and pedagogical expertise of the instructor of record will be required. This must not be abandoned falsely in the name of community. In what may seem a paradox, a successful educational community of inquiry is very much dependent upon direct instruction.

Managing discourse in face-to-face and online environments presents different challenges. In face-to-face discussion, time is a precious element that may demand vigilant monitoring and management depending on the particular task. In plenary discussions, it may be advantageous for the instructor to take a lead role in managing and modeling discourse. In breakout groups, however, participants should be expected to assume greater responsibility for facilitating and directing the discussion. On the other hand, the reflective nature of online discourse may require participants to take a greater role in directing the discussion. This is a great opportunity for participants to develop these essential abilities. This should not, however, be in the total absence of the instructor. In either case, participants need to have some awareness of the goals of the task and the time constraints.

Direct instruction plays an important role in enhancing metacognitive awareness and action. Sharing the thought processes of a discipline expert will reveal reflective processes and model discourse. At the outset, students need to be introduced to the inquiry process to increase their awareness of the inquiry process and discuss why it is important to monitor and manage learning.

Akyol and Garrison (2011a) provide a metacognitive construct consisting of knowledge, monitoring, and regulation of cognition contextualized within the Community of Inquiry framework. They also report, "Students became metacognitively mature through explaining, questioning, clarifying, justifying or providing strategies reciprocally within a community of inquiry" (p. 188). Metacognition begins with the knowledge or awareness of metacognition. Monitoring (assessment) and managing (planning) learning requires that students be provided with a conceptual understanding as well as a model of discourse for deep and meaningful thinking and learning. In turn, the likelihood of moving through the inquiry stages will be greatly enhanced when participants have this metacognitive awareness and are encouraged to assume responsibility for developing, monitoring and managing abilities.

Metacognition, however, is challenging in a community of inquiry, as we must consider individual and shared monitoring and regulation. As Akyol and Garrison (2011a) suggest, "Metacognition in an online learning community is defined as the set of higher knowledge and skills to monitor and regulate manifest cognitive processes of *self and others* [emphasis added]" (p. 184). Metacognition requires feedback and this responsibility must be shared through discourse. This once again points to the collaborative and distributive nature of teaching presence, including direct instruction. Students must be encouraged to explain their thinking and, strategically, how it will facilitate achieving resolution. Practices that can improve metacognitive abilities are peer assessments, collective reflection, and modeling metacognitive processes. Journals may be helpful to encourage students to reflect metacognitively on the learning process. It may also be advantageous for students to monitor and manage topics of discussion formally.

With regard to having students formally monitor their participation in online discussion, several strategies can be utilized by a course instructor. For example, students could be required to use the practical inquiry model to self-code their discussion postings for cognitive presence using the information presented in Table 4.3.

TABLE 4.3. Practical inquiry model for self-coding discussion forum postings

PHASE	DESCRIPTION
Triggering event	This phase initiates the inquiry process through a well-thought-out activity to ensure full engagement and buy-in from the students. This has several positive outcomes in terms of involving students, assessing the state of knowledge, and generating unintended but constructive ideas.
Exploration	This phase focuses first on understanding the nature of the problem and then searching for relevant information and possible explanations.

PHASE	DESCRIPTION
Integration	This phase moves into a more focused and structured phase of constructing meaning. Decisions are made about the integration of ideas and how order can be created parsimoniously.
Resolution	This phase is the resolution of the dilemma or problem, whether that is reducing complexity by constructing a meaningful framework or discovering a contextually specific solution. This confirmation or testing phase may be accomplished by direct or vicarious action.

Another strategy is to co-create a discussion grading rubric with the students so that they can self-assess the quality of their postings. Table 4.4 provides an example of a discussion forum rubric that can be used to achieve this goal.

TABLE 4.4. Discussion forum rubric

POINTS	INERPRETATION	GRADING CRITERIA
4	Excellent (A)	The posting is accurate, original, relevant; it teaches us something new and is well written. Four-point comments add substantial teaching presence to the course, and stimulate additional thought about the issue under discussion.
3	Above average (B)	The posting lacks at least one of the above qualities, but is above average quality. A three-point comment makes a significant contribution to our understanding of the issue being discussed.
2	Average (C)	The comment lacks two or three of the required qualities. Comments that are based upon personal opinion or personal experience often fall within this category.
1	Minimal (D)	The comment presents little or no new information. However, one-point comments may provide social presence and contribute to a collegial atmosphere.

POINTS	INTERPRETATION	GRADING CRITERIA
0	Unacceptable (F)	The comment adds no value to the discussion.
No penalty	Excellent subject field	The subject field conveys the main point of the posting. The reader clearly understands the main point of the posting before reading it.
1-point penalty	Minimal subject field	The subject field provides key word(s) only. The reader knows the general area with which the posting deals.
2-point penalty	Unacceptable subject field	The subject field provides little or no information about the posting.

Adapted from Pelz (2004)

Student-moderated discussions can also be effective for the development of metacognitive skills. Several approaches can be used to ensure that this is a successful learning activity.

First, we recommend that the instructor moderate the first online discussion in a course. This way the instructor can demonstrate, model, and debrief about the expected requirements for a discussion moderator.

Second, it is important to provide students with clear and detailed instructions about their roles as moderator. Table 4.5 provides an example for the moderation of an online discussion about a textbook chapter.

TABLE 4.5. Student-moderated discussion instructions

CRITERIA	DESCRIPTION
Overview	Write a discussion question from this chapter of the textbook. Read the questions already posted, and do not repeat a question asked by another student. Your question should relate directly to an issue discussed in the text and should require a thoughtful response. Don't ask a question that can be answered by looking up the answer in the textbook. Attitude, opinion, and application questions usually get thoughtful responses.

CRITERIA	DESCRIPTION
Instructions	Participation in a student-led discussion consists of the following four steps:
	1. Post your original question. This must be done within the first two days the module is active. This will be your thread – you will be the discussion leader. Your job is to facilitate this discussion and get as much information from the other participants as you can that relates to the question you have asked.
	2. Read the questions posted by the other students, and respond to at least three of them. Choose the threads you think will be the most interesting and beneficial to you. You will be a participant in these threads.
	3. Respond to every student who responds to you. Do this in your own thread as well as the other threads in which you are participating.
	4. Continue participating in the threads until the module is over.
Additional note	If other students are not participating in your thread, perhaps it is because your question is too complex, confusing, or uninteresting. In this case, substitute another question.

Adapted from Pelz (2004)

Third, in order to reflect upon and document the learning that took place in an online discussion, we encourage student moderators to create a summary of the discussion. In order to facilitate this process we again recommend the use of the practical inquiry model. Table 4.6 illustrates how this model can be used to guide the development of these summaries and in chapter 6 we will demonstrate how various types of technologies can be used to support this process (e.g., wikis).

TABLE 4.6. Practical inquiry model for online discussion summaries

PHASE	KEY QUESTIONS
Triggering events	What were the key questions or issues identified in the discussion?
Exploration	What opportunities and challenges were discussed?
Integration	What recommendations and conclusions can you draw from the discussion?
Resolution/application	How can we apply the lessons learned from this discussion to our course assignments and future career plans?
Key resources	What can we use to find further information and ideas about this topic (e.g., websites, articles, books)?

CONCLUSION

In summary, we must be vigilant that neither too much nor too little direct instruction is present. Too much direct instruction will very quickly discourage participation and reduce proposing new ideas or solutions. Too little direct instruction risks moving to resolution and, like too much direction, will shut down participation and discourse.

5 Assessment

If we wish to discover the truth about an educational system, we must look into its assessment procedures. (Rowntree, 1977, p. 1)

INTRODUCTION

The term *assessment* in higher education often conjures up different sentiments and emotions. From an instructor perspective, Ramsden (2003) states that assessment involves "getting to know our students and the quality of their learning" (p.180). Conversely, students in a recent study were asked to use one word to describe their perceptions of assessment (Vaughan, 2010b). The four most common words were: *fear, stress, anxiety,* and *judgment.* This disconnect between instructor and student perceptions regarding assessment is a serious issue, especially since a number of educational researchers have clearly linked student approaches to learning with the design and associated feedback of an assessment activity

(Biggs, 1998; Hedberg & Corrent-Agostinho, 1999; Marton & Saljo, 1984: Ramsden, 2003; Thistlethwaite, 2006). For example, standardized tests with minimal feedback can lead to memorization and a surface approach to learning, while collaborative group projects can encourage dialogue, richer forms of feedback, and deeper modes of learning (Entwistle, 2000). The purpose of this chapter is to demonstrate how the Community of Inquiry (CoI) framework can be applied to blended learning environments in order to create meaningful assessment activities for students in higher education.

PRINCIPLES OF ASSESSMENT

Over time, there has been an increased emphasis on formative assessment practices (Gorsky, Caspi, & Trumper, 2006; Gibbs & Simpson 2004, Gibbs, 2006; and American Association of Higher Education and Accreditation, 1996). Pask's (1976) Conversation Theory of Learning suggests that learning takes place through our intrapersonal (inner voice) and interpersonal (external voice with others) conversations and that formative assessment practices help to shape and regulate this dialogue in higher education courses. Nicol and Macfarlane-Dick (2006) have developed the following seven principles of good assessment feedback based on the work of Pask:

Good feedback:
1. helps to clarify what good performance is (goals, criteria, standards)
2. facilitates the development of self-assessment and reflection in learning
3. delivers high quality information to students about their learning
4. encourages teacher and peer dialogue around learning
5. encourages positive motivational beliefs and self-esteem

6. provides opportunities to close the gap between current and desired performance

7. provides information to instructors that can be used to help shape teaching

These assessment principles clearly align with the concept of an educational community of inquiry, which is "composed of a group of individuals who collaboratively engage in purposeful critical discourse and reflection to construct personal meaning and confirm mutual understanding" (Garrison, 2011, p. 15). When such a community takes place in a blended learning environment there are a variety of opportunities for self-, peer-, and instructor-assessment feedback.

SELF-ASSESSMENT

Alverno College (2006) defines *self-assessment* feedback as "the ability of students to observe, analyze, and judge their own performances on the basis of criteria and to determine how they can improve" (p.1). Akyol and Garrison (2011a) have recently demonstrated how this notion of self-regulated learning or metacognition "in a community of inquiry is a collaborative process where internal and external conditions are being constantly assessed" (p. 184). In addition, they have described three dimensions of metacognition, which involve the knowledge, monitoring, and regulation of cognition. The knowledge of cognition refers to awareness of self as a learner and includes entering knowledge and motivation associated with the inquiry process, academic discipline, and expectancies. The monitoring of cognition dimension implies the awareness and willingness to reflect upon the learning process. And, the regulation of metacognition focuses on the action dimension of the learning experience, which involves the employment of strategies to achieve meaningful learning outcomes.

Self-assessment activities that utilize rubrics and online journals can be used to support this metacognitive process in a blended learning environment.

The Teaching, Learning, and Technology (TLT) Group (2011) define *rubric* as "an explicit set of criteria used for assessing a particular type of work or performance. A rubric usually also includes levels of potential achievement for each criterion, and sometimes also includes work or performance samples that typify each of those levels" (n.p.). In a blended community of inquiry, rubrics can be useful for clarifying assignment and assessment expectations only when students are actively involved in their co-construction. Students in a pre-service teacher education course indicated that without student involvement rubrics "can become simple checklists, a way to make sure that you've covered everything the teacher wants for the assignment rather than what you really wanted to do and learn" (Vaughan, 2010b, p. 11). Unfortunately, this comment suggests that without student involvement rubrics have the potential to support a surface rather than a deep approach to learning.

Several types of digital technologies can be used to support the co-construction of assessment rubrics in a community of inquiry. These include applications such as Rubistar (http://rubistar.4teachers.org/index.php), Teachnology (http://www.teachnology.com/web_tools/rubrics/), and Google Drive (https://drive.google.com/). An example of a co-constructed assessment rubric for a lesson plan assignment is illustrated in Figure 5.1.

In addition, students should be provided with the opportunity to practice applying the co-constructed rubric to student work completed in previous course sections, and in order to take ownership for the rubric they should be provided with the ability to add one unique grading component or criteria (e.g., creativity).

Assessment rubric for your lesson plan assignment:

Component	Beginning	Developing	Accomplished	Self-Assessment Comments	Peer Comments	Teacher Comments
Peer Review	0.25 points *Incomplete peer review of another student's lesson plan*	0.5 points *Basic* comments regarding: What you learned from reviewing this lesson plan? What you liked about this lesson plan? What recommendations or advice you shared with your colleague to help improve this lesson plan?	1.0 points *Substantive* and *reflective* comments about what you learned from reviewing another student's lesson plan, what you liked about the plan, and suggestions for improving this document.			
Self-Reflection	0.25 points *Incomplete* self-reflection of the lesson plan assignment	0.5 points Completed self-reflection scoring of the lesson plan assignment with *basic* comments for each component	1.0 points Completed self-reflection scoring of the lesson plan assignment with *substantive* and *reflective* comments about each component			
Subject/Age Appropriate	0 point The lesson plan is *not connected* to an Alberta Education subject area and there is no indication of a target grade level.	0.5 point There is *some indication* of a connection to an Alberta Education subject area and grade level.	1.0 points There is a *clear connection* to an Alberta Education subject area and the content of the lesson is age appropriate (i.e. Division 1, 2, 3 or 4).			
Resources	0 point There is no *indication* of the resources required to complete this lesson plan	0.5 point There is a *partially* developed list of resources required to complete this lesson plan.	1.0 point There is a *fully developed* list of resources required to complete this lesson plan *including* Web site titles and URLs, computer hardware and software requirements			

FIGURE 5.1.   Co-constructed assessment rubric for a lesson plan
assignment (http://tinyurl.com/lessonplanrubric)

Digital technologies can be also be used in a blended environment to
provide a variety of options for students to assess themselves. For
example, students can use Audacity (http://audacity.sourceforge.
net/), an open-source audio tool, to create self-assessment narra-
tions of how they achieved the various learning outcomes outlined
in the rubric. The use of self-assessment audio feedback can be a
powerful way for students to internalize their learning (Ice, Curtis,
Phillips, & Wells, 2007).

Students in professional programs such as teacher education and nursing are often required to maintain either a course or program journal. Online blogging tools such as WordPress (http://wordpress.org/) and Google's Blogger (www.blogger.com/) are commonly being used to support this type of self-assessment activity. Figure 5.2 provides an example of a student's online journal posting about a lesson plan assignment.

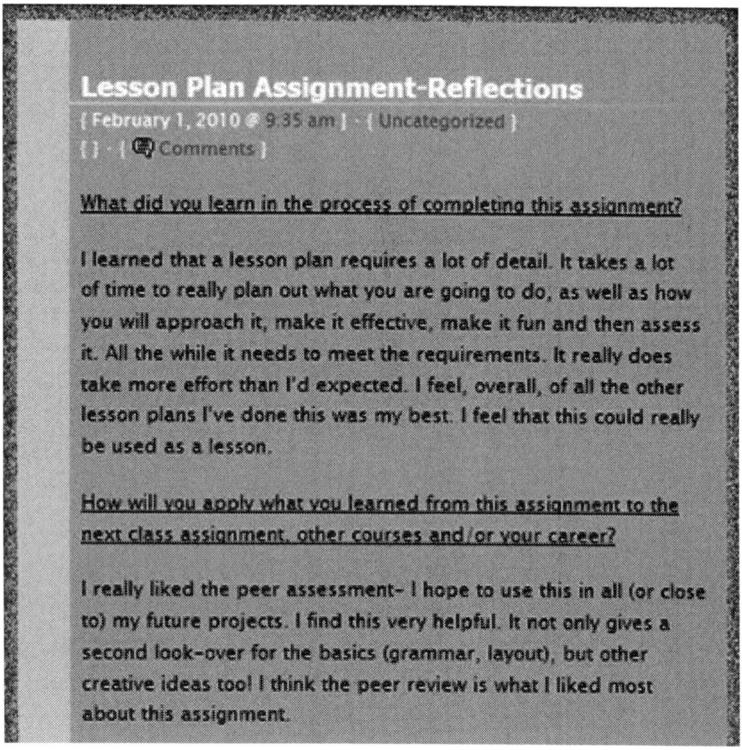

Lesson Plan Assignment-Reflections

{ February 1, 2010 @ 9:35 am } · { Uncategorized }
{ } · { 🖳 Comments }

What did you learn in the process of completing this assignment?

I learned that a lesson plan requires a lot of detail. It takes a lot of time to really plan out what you are going to do, as well as how you will approach it, make it effective, make it fun and then assess it. All the while it needs to meet the requirements. It really does take more effort than I'd expected. I feel, overall, of all the other lesson plans I've done this was my best. I feel that this could really be used as a lesson.

How will you apply what you learned from this assignment to the next class assignment, other courses and/or your career?

I really liked the peer assessment— I hope to use this in all (or close to) my future projects. I find this very helpful. It not only gives a second look-over for the basics (grammar, layout), but other creative ideas too! I think the peer review is what I liked most about this assignment.

FIGURE 5.2. Example of an online journal posting with guiding questions

Students in a teacher education program suggested that online journals can be useful for self-reflection but, as one wrote, too often they can become a "boring and repetitive activity when I am simply being asked to reply to a set of teacher directed questions. Usually, I just post what I think the teacher wants to hear not what I'm really thinking" (Vaughan, 2010b, p. 12). Again, without student involvement, this type of self-assessment activity can reinforce a surface rather than a deep approach to learning.

In a blended community of inquiry, students should be provided with a high degree of control over their online journal postings in order for them to discuss and develop their own metacognitive strategies. This can be achieved by designing online journal assignments focused on process-orientated postings that lead to a final product such as an end of the semester self-reflection paper. This paper can then be assessed by the instructor using a rubric that has been co-constructed with the students in a digital format such as Google Drive.

PEER ASSESSMENT

The Foundation Coalition (2002) indicates, "Peer assessment allows students to assess other students (their peers) in a course. Peer assessment can also provide data that might be used in assigning individual grades for team assignments" (p. 1). The French moralist and essayist Joubert (1842) is attributed with the quote: "To teach is to learn twice," and in an effective community of inquiry all participants are both learners and teachers. The term teaching presence, rather than teacher presence, implies that everyone in the community is responsible for providing input on the design, facilitation, and direction of the teaching process.

In a blended community of inquiry, one of the biggest challenges of peer assessment activities can be finding a convenient place and time for all students to meet outside of the classroom. Digital technologies can be used to overcome this barrier, beginning with the group areas in learning management systems such as Blackboard. These group areas can be used to communicate and share documents about the peer assessment process for individual and group projects. They usually consist of asynchronous (e.g., e-mail and discussion board) and synchronous (e.g., chat) communication tools, along with a file exchange function.

Collaborative writing tools such as Google Drive can also be used to provide meaningful peer review feedback on written assignments (Figure 5.3). This application allows students to control who has commenting and editing privileges for their documents.

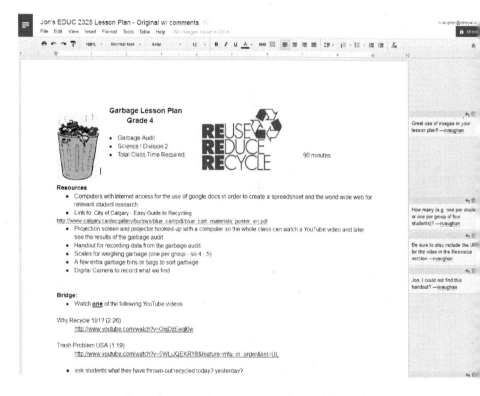

FIGURE 5.3. Example peer review comments for a writing assignment in Google Drive

In addition, online journal applications such as Blogger can be used to provide peer review feedback on individual project work (Figure 5.4).

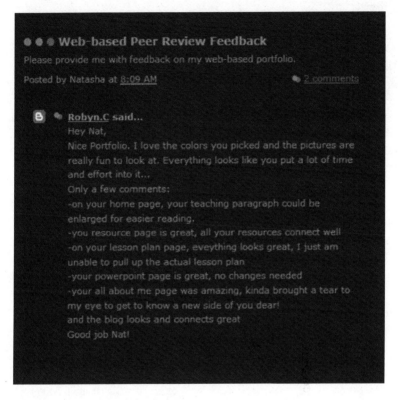

FIGURE 5.4. Peer review of individual project work using Google's Blogger application

Additionally, wiki tools such as Wikispaces can be used to co-create and critique online discussion summaries (Figure 5.5). The history files of a wiki summary clearly demonstrate the contribution and critique that was made by each member of the group.

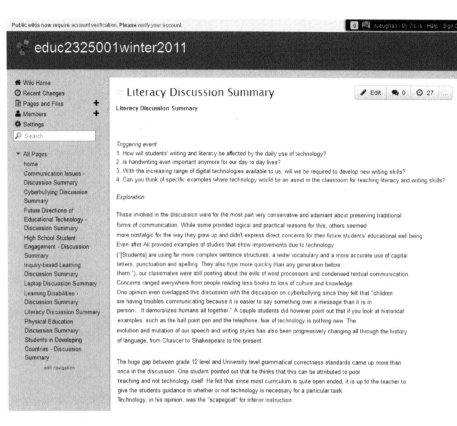

FIGURE 5.5. Group online discussion summary and critique in Wikispaces

Digital tools such as the University of California at Los Angeles' Calibrated Peer Review (CPR) (http://cpr.molsci.ucla.edu/) have also been developed to help students learn how to provide constructive feedback to their peers in a community of inquiry.

Within classroom settings, personal response systems (e.g., clickers) can be used to support a form of peer instruction (Crouch & Mazur, 2001). The process begins with the teacher posing a question or problem. The students initially work individually toward a solution and vote on what they believe is the correct answer by selecting the desired numbered or lettered response on their clicker.

The results are then projected for the entire class to view. For a good question, there is usually a broad range of responses. Students are then required to compare and discuss their solutions with the person next to them in the classroom in order to come to a consensus. Another vote is taken but this time only one response or clicker per group can be utilized. In most circumstances, the range of responses decreases and usually centers on the correct answer. As an alternative to this process in a community of inquiry, the instructor can provide groups of students with opportunities to generate the quiz questions in advance of the classroom session.

While digital technologies can provide students with increased flexibility and communication opportunities to complete peer assessment activities, outside of the classroom several additional concerns have been expressed. First, students often lack previous experience with peer assessment; they strongly recommend that in a community of inquiry instructors should "provide guidance and a class orientation on how to give each other meaningful feedback and that there should be opportunities for both written and oral peer feedback" (Vaughan, 2010b, p. 18). In a blended learning environment, these students also suggest that instructors should "provide class time to begin and conclude peer assessment activities in order to build trust and accountability for the peer assessment process" (Vaughan, 2010b, p. 19).

INSTRUCTOR ASSESSMENT

Instructor assessment practices in higher education are often limited to high-stakes summative assessment activities such as midterm and final examinations (Boud, 2000). The role of an instructor in a community of inquiry is to provide ongoing and meaningful assessment feedback in order to help students develop the necessary metacognitive skills and strategies to take responsibility for their own learning.

In a blended environment, an instructor can use a variety of digital technologies to provide diagnostic, formative, and summative assessment to students in a community of inquiry. For example, instructors can use collaborative writing tools to provide formative assessment feedback at checkpoints or milestones for individual or group projects (Figure 5.6). This allows students to receive instructor feedback throughout the process of constructing the project rather than just focusing on summative assessment feedback for the final product.

Darren's Lesson Plan

Lesson title :
- Golf/Phys-Ed/Grade 10-12 Div 4
- 1 hour 20 minutes

Resources
- Laptops with internet access per every 2 students
- Video Camera- per every 2 students
- Golf Clubs
- Wiffle·balls
- Gym
- http://www.youtube.com/watch?v=nESDTgMckOU

Bridge:
Watch Youtube video of Tiger Woods taking a golf swing in slow motion (Youtube search slow motion golf swing- will be first to appear) 1-2 minutes.http://www.youtube.com/watch?v=nESDTgMckOU Be sure to also put this web site in your resource section -Norm Vaughan 1/24/10 11:02 PM

Learning outcomes :
- This lesson will allow students to identify the areas of their golf swing that needs improvement.
- P3 4.1 and 4.2 You also need to write out the text for this Alberta ICT Learning Outcome :) -Norm Vaughan 1/24/10 11:02 PM

FIGURE 5.6. Example of using Google Drive to provide instructor formative assessment feedback comments

Instructors in a blended community of inquiry are also encouraged to take a portfolio approach to assessment. This involves students receiving a second chance or opportunity for summative assessment on their course assignments. For example, students initially submit and receive instructor assessment for each of the required course assignments. Throughout the semester, students then have the opportunity to revise these assignments based on the initial instructor feedback and to post them to their course or program portfolios for final summative assessment by the instructor. A range of e-Portfolio tools can support this process, ranging from the LiveText commercial application (https://www.livetext.com/) to the free Google Sites tool (http://sites.google.com/).

In addition, digital technologies can be used to support external expert assessment opportunities. For example, students can publically share critiques of academic articles by using blogging tools such as WordPress and Blogger. The authors of these articles can then be invited to post comments about these critiques to the students' blogs. Blogging applications will be described in more detail in chapter 6.

External experts can also provide assessment feedback on individual or group presentations through the use of web-based video technologies. These types of presentations can be video recorded and either streamed live (e.g., Livestream at http://www.livestream.com/) or posted to a video-sharing site such as YouTube (http://www.youtube.com/). The external experts can then provide assessment feedback in either synchronous (e.g., real-time audio) or asynchronous formats (e.g., online discussion forums) to the students.

In terms of strategies, students in the teacher education program study suggested that instructors should "focus on providing students with ongoing formative assessment feedback rather than on just summative midterm and final examination comments" (Vaughan, 2010b, p. 22). They also recommended that instructors should strive to "provide oral feedback in addition to their written assessment feedback. For example, instructors could request that students meet with them during office hour sessions to orally debrief about assignments" (Vaughan, 2010b, p. 22). Finally, these students emphasized, "Let us provide instructors with more feedback on their assignments and teaching practice throughout the semester, not just at the end – assessment should be a two-way conversation between students and instructors" (Vaughan, 2010b, p. 22).

CONCLUSION

Self, peer, and instructor assessment should be an integrated process in a blended community of inquiry, rather than a series of isolated events, in order to help students develop their own metacognitive skills and strategies. For example, a student in the teacher education study commented, "I used the self-reflection for checking my work and making sure I had everything I needed. I used peer review for a different perspective on my work, and I used instructor feedback to understand how I could improve my work" (Vaughan, 2010b, p. 23). Another student in the same study stated, "Self-reflection showed me what I liked about my work and what needed to be improved, peer feedback gave comments on what could be done better and then instructor feedback gave ideas on how the assignment could be fixed up to get a better mark" (Vaughan, 2010b, p. 23).

In addition, these students stressed how a blended Community of Inquiry framework supported by digital technologies helped them integrate these three forms of assessment into a triad approach (Figure 5.7).

This triad-approach involves students using rubrics, blogs, and online quizzes to provide themselves with self-reflection and feedback on their course assignments. They can then receive further peer feedback on their course work via the use of digital technologies such wikis, clickers, and other peer review tools. Finally, instructors and in some cases external experts can review students' ePortfolios and use digital video technologies to observe student performance, diagnose student misconceptions, and provide additional assessment feedback.

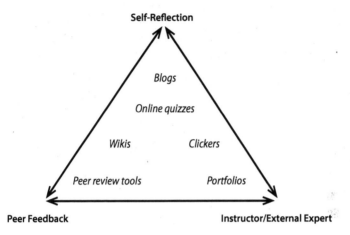

FIGURE 5.7. Using digital technologies to support a triad approach to assessement in a blended community of inquiry

An international call for a greater focus on assessment *for* learning, rather than on assessment for *just* measurement and accountability of student performance, is well documented in the educational research literature (Yeh, 2009). The use of digital technologies to support student assessment in a blended community of inquiry may lead to Hattie's (2009) vision of a visible teaching and learning framework where "teachers SEE learning through the eyes of their students and students SEE themselves as their own teachers" (p. 238).

6 Technology

When I see the power that technology gives us in terms of the new ways of collaborating and sharing, and the quality of the resources that people are sharing, I think it's just changing everything. (Tinney, 2013)

INTRODUCTION

The purpose of this chapter is to describe how digital technologies and educational strategies can be used to design, facilitate, and direct collaborative communities of inquiry. We begin this chapter with an overview of collaborative learning, followed by descriptions of how various types of technologies can be used to design, facilitate, and direct a blended learning environment in higher education.

Sustained collaboration in the construction and confirmation of knowledge represents a new era in educational practice. The New Media Consortium and the EDUCAUSE Learning Initiative's 2010

Horizon Report (Johnson, Levine, Smith, & Stone, 2010) identifies how the "work of students is increasingly seen as collaborative by nature . . . the emergence of a raft of new (and often free) tools has made collaboration easier than at any other point in history" (p. 4). They identify collaboration and communication as a significant trend in expanding the possibilities for learning and creativity. A significant driver of this transformation in learning has been the emergence of social media technologies.

These technologies present exciting opportunities, but the challenge is in understanding the educational design and pedagogical issues associated with the best use of social media tools such as blogs, wikis, online communities and synchronous communication technologies (e.g., Adobe Connect). The true potential of these tools is in the design, facilitation, and direction of synchronous and asynchronous communities of inquiry that support worthwhile educational goals and higher-order learning activities.

We believe that all of education is experiencing a transformative shift from issues of accessing and sharing information to designing communities of inquiry where participants are actively engaged in deep and meaningful learning. Social media applications are about using the Web in a way that capitalizes on its greatest asset: bringing people together in learning communities where participants (students and teachers in the case of education) with a common interest can interact and collaborate on purposeful activities. Brown and Adler (2008) argue that the capabilities of social media tools have "shifted attention from access to information toward access to people" (p. 18). These applications allow people to come together in collaborative learning communities.

An educational community of inquiry is a group of individuals who collaboratively engage in purposeful critical discourse and reflection to construct personal meaning and confirm mutual understanding (Garrison, 2011). Historically, this has been the ideal of learning environments in higher education. Only in the last half-century, with the growth of enrolment in higher education, has the practice been diminished as a result of larger classes and passive lectures. As social media tools continue to emerge and evolve, educators are presented with the opportunity to realize the historical ideal of higher education to learn in collaborative communities of inquiry.

COLLABORATION

Social media applications have the potential to support collaborative learning activities. In order to achieve this objective we must first step back and rethink what we are doing. What are the core values of an educational experience and how can we align our assessment activities and learning outcomes with the need for creative and innovative graduates that can work productively in collaborative environments? To help address these challenges, educators are increasingly coming to understand that we must provide more interactive and engaged learning experiences (Barkley, 2009; Kuh, Kinzie, Scuh, Whitt, & Associates, 2005). The key to engaging learners in deep and meaningful learning is through collaborative communities of inquiry — not the passive lecture approach that currently dominates higher education. As mentioned previously, engagement in collaborative discourse and reflection has historically been the hallmark of higher education. Social media tools can be used as a catalyst to redesign our blended courses for more active and collaborative learning experiences. Our first lesson is to avoid simply layering these digital tools onto a deficient educational design (e.g., information transfer model, which only focuses on the presentation and organization of content).

Collaborative communities of inquiry are characterized by sharing personal meaning and the validation of understanding through discourse (Garrison, 2011). Philosophically, this approach to learning is founded in the tradition of social-constructivist learning theory. Students are expected to assume the individual responsibility to make sense of new concepts and ideas but with the support and feedback of a collaborative community of peers and mentors. Inquiry is at the core of a collaborative learning experience. A wide range of social media applications is available to support a collaborative inquiry approach to learning in a blended course.

SOCIAL MEDIA APPLICATIONS AND EDUCATIONAL STRATEGIES

Tim O'Reilly (2005) is credited with coining the term *Web 2.0* to describe the trend in the use of Web technology and design that aims to enhance creativity, information sharing, and, most notably, collaboration among users. Recently, this concept has been defined as *social media*: "a group of Internet-based applications that build on the ideological and technological foundations of Web 2.0" (Kaplan & Haenlein, 2010, p. 60). These applications can be used to support collaborative learning in a variety of formats. For example, social bookmarking applications can be used to share personal collections of Web-based resources to complete group projects. Blogs can facilitate student self-reflection and peer review of course assignments. Students can use wikis to summarize course discussions collaboratively, refine research papers, or even co-create online books. Social networking systems (SNS) such as Facebook and LinkedIn can be used to extend the boundaries of the classroom to create online communities and discussions and debates that include past students, potential employers, and subject matter experts. Audio, graphic, and video files can now be created and shared through social content applications such as PodOmatic, Flikr, and YouTube. These files and other data sources can then be recombined to create new meaning and interpretations by using mashup applications such as Intel's Mash Maker and Yahoo Pipes. Synchronous communication technologies such as Skype and Adobe Connect allow students to communicate and collaborate outside of the classroom in real time.

Moreover, virtual world applications such as Second Life provide opportunities for rich synchronous interaction in 3-D immersive worlds to support collaborative and creative project-based work. We will now examine how the following eight categories of social media applications can be used to design, facilitate, and direct collaborative learning activities in blended courses and programs.

1. social bookmarking
2. blogs
3. wikis
4. social networking
5. social content
6. mashups
7. synchronous communication and conferencing
8. virtual worlds

Additional examples of social media applications and ideas for collaborative learning activities are provided on a corresponding wiki site (http://tinyurl.com/collaborativecommunity).

SOCIAL BOOKMARKING

The general idea behind social bookmarking is that, rather than saving a bookmark for a Web page in a browser such as Internet Explorer or Firefox, users instead save the bookmark to a publicly accessible website (e.g., delicious.com). Other people can then see the bookmark and, ideally, be exposed to something that they wouldn't otherwise encounter. In addition, some social bookmarking sites also employ a voting system that allows users to indicate what bookmarks they found interesting (e.g., reddit.com). As a bookmark receives more and more votes, its prominence on the website increases, which in turn attracts more and more votes. The ultimate goal is to have the bookmark appear on the home page of the social bookmarking site.

This ability to share and build upon the resources of others can help to develop relationships between concepts and people in a higher education course or program. Social bookmarking applications can be used for student-generated course reading lists, debates, individual, and group projects.

COURSE READING LISTS AND ASSIGNMENTS

For example, rather than having a predetermined reading list, at the beginning of each semester, an instructor could assign student groups to find resources related to specific course concepts or issues. These resources can then be shared and annotated by using a social bookmarking tool such as diigo.com (Figure 6.1).

These resources can also be used for pre-class reading assignments. Traditionally, this activity involved a reading from the course textbook. Social bookmarking systems such as citeULike and Edtags can now be used to provide students with access to relevant and engaging Web-based articles and resources.

Despite the ability to access relevant learning material easily, the common challenge still exists of getting students to engage meaningfully in pre-class activities. Novak, Patterson, Gavrin, and Christian (1999) have used a survey or quiz tool to create triggering events for students in advance of a synchronous session. They have coined the term *Just-in-Time Teaching* (JiTT) to describe the process of getting students to read a Web-based article and then respond to an online survey or quiz, shortly before a class. The instructor then reviews the student submissions "just-in-time" to adjust the subsequent class session in order to address the students' needs, identified by the survey or quiz results. A typical survey or quiz consists of four concept-based questions with the final question asking students: "What did you not understand about the required reading and what would you like me [the instructor] to focus on within the next synchronous session?"

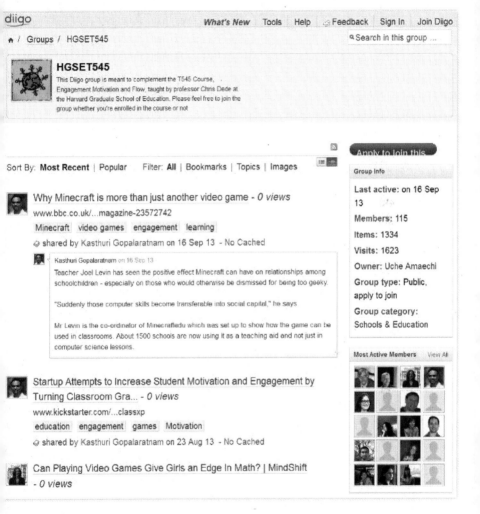

FIGURE 6.1. Co-constructed course reading list in Diigo

Educational research has demonstrated that in-class and online debates are an effective way to engage students in deeper approaches to learning (Kanuka, 2005). Students can use a social bookmarking application such as Social Bookmarking to collect and annotate resources for debate activities.

For example, in a blended course, student teams could be assigned to collect a series of resources that support a particular position or ideology, outside of class time. During class, students can then be asked to take the opposite side of the debate and use the resources collected by the other student teams to prepare their arguments.

INDIVIDUAL AND GROUP PROJECTS

Social bookmarking systems such as Delicious enable students to create their own personal libraries, which they can then share with their colleagues. The advantage of using such a service is that students are continually able to build and share their resource collections throughout their university experiences. This allows the students to make intentional connections between projects and assignments that they complete in different courses.

BLOGS

A *blog* is a Web-based personal journal with reflections, comments, and, often, hyperlinks to other blogs that the author of the site visits on a regular basis (Downes, 2004). People can subscribe to blogs by using a Really Simple Syndication (RSS) feed to receive automated content updates. Blogging can provide students with opportunities to receive external feedback and to make contributions to the dialogues in their fields of study. In blended learning courses, blogs can be used to support self-reflection and peer review of course assignments, allowing students to take a deeper approach to their learning by going public with their work (Vaughan, 2008).

SELF-REFLECTION

At the beginning of the semester, an instructor can require each student to create a blog using applications such as Blogger and WordPress. Students can use these blogs to document their learning growth and development throughout the term. For example, during the first week of classes students post an initial journal entry about their personal learning goals for the course and what they think they already know about the course concepts. Then at the end of the course, students create a final journal entry that reflects on what they have learned and how they have changed, grown, and developed throughout the course.

Blogs can also be used to get students to self-reflect about their course assignments. The purpose of these entries is to have students intentionally reflect about what they learned through the process of completing the assessment activity and how they could apply this learning to their future course studies or careers. The following questions can be used to guide this activity:

1. What did you learn in the process of completing this assignment?
2. How will you apply what you learned from this assignment to the next class assignment, other courses, and/or your career?

PEER REVIEW

A peer review process can also be supported through the use of blogs. Students can post drafts of course assignments to their blogs and then their peers can review these documents and post comments to the author's blog (Figure 6.2).

Guiding questions for this peer review process could include:

1. What did you learn from reviewing this document?
2. What were the strengths (e.g., content, writing style, format, and structure) of the document?
3. What constructive advice and/or recommendations could you provide for improving the quality of this document?

WIKIS

A wiki is a collection of web pages that can be edited by anyone, at any time, from anywhere. The possibilities for using wikis as a platform for collaborative projects are limited only by one's imagination and time (Leuf & Cunningham, 2001). In blended learning courses students can use wikis collaboratively to create course notes, online discussion summaries, group essays, and even course textbooks.

COURSE NOTES

Many students in higher education are now bringing laptop computers to class, and wiki applications such as Google Drive and TitanPad can be used to co-construct a set of course notes. This can either be an individual activity or the instructor can assign student teams the task of creating notes for specific class periods.

The advantage of using an application such as TitanPad is that students can work simultaneously on the same document without overwriting each other's work. Students can also assign a specific text colour to their wiki contributions in order to keep track of their own work.

Nikki's UC Blog

a UCalgaryBlogs.ca site

Home   Sample Page

— Blended Learning EDER679.20 -Learning Goals   Course Redesign Proposal —   [   ] Search

Article Critique – The present state and future trends of blended learning in workspace learning settings across five countries

Posted on 23 January, 2013 by Nikki Mountford

The article focuses the current and future status and trends of workplace learning in relation to blended learning across 5 diverse countries and cultures; China, South Korea, Taiwan, United States and the United Kingdom. This study is intended to provide a marker in corporate training settings for direction and validity or intensity of blended learning. There is a focus around four main points; how is blended learning perceived and practiced in workplace settings, what are the benefits and barriers, are there cross-cultural differences and what are common and emerging strategies for blended learning (Kim, Bonk, & Teng, 2009, p. 300).

Recent Posts

- Toolkit 1: Parent Advocacy Brief: A Parent's Guide to Universal Design for Learning (UDL)
- Toolkit #2 – Accessibility: A Guide for Educators
- Toolkit #1 – Index for Inclusion
- eLearning Consortia
- D2L – not just another LMS

Recent Comments

- Alan Stephen on eLearning Consortia
- drdoug on D2L – not just another LMS

One Response to *Article Critique – The present state and future trends of blended learning in workspace learning settings across five countries*

Kim *says:*
30 January, 2013 at 10:17 am

Hi Nikki,

Your article summary is detailed and thorough. The article was well selected in that it is relevant to your present working situation and is therefore highly personally motivating for you. I am curious about your statement that you are, 'building a learning institution'. Does this mean more than you are working towards providing a blended learning approach for your current institution? Some clarification in your critique, around this point, would be useful. I wonder what the impact will be in your workplace, Nikki, once a blended learning / working environment is created and implemented.

FIGURE 6.2. Peer review of a blog posting of an article critique

Student-moderated online discussion forums can be used to promote individual reflection and critical dialogue between face-to-face
sessions in a blended learning course. For example, at the beginning
of the semester, groups of students (three to five) can self-select
a topic that is related to key course concepts and/or issues. Each
group is responsible for moderating and summarizing their selected
online discussion for a set period of time (often one or two weeks).
Students can use Garrison, Anderson, and Archer's (2001) practical
inquiry model as a guide to create reflective discussion summaries.
For example:

1. Triggering events – What were the key questions
   identified this week?
2. Exploration – What opportunities and challenges were
   discussed?
3. Integration – What recommendations and conclusions
   can you draw from the discussion?
4. Resolution/application – How can we apply the "lessons
   learned" from this discussion to our course assignments
   and future career plans?
5. Key resources (e.g., websites, articles, books) that we could
   use to find further information and ideas about this topic?

A wiki can then be used to draft notes and a final summary (synthesis and analysis) of the online discussion based on these questions
or additional guidelines that are co-created by the students and the
course teacher (see Figure 6.3).

Wikis can provide a collaborative workspace for students to
construct group essays. The advantage of using an application such
as Google Drive is that students can access these group documents
from any computer or mobile device with Internet access.

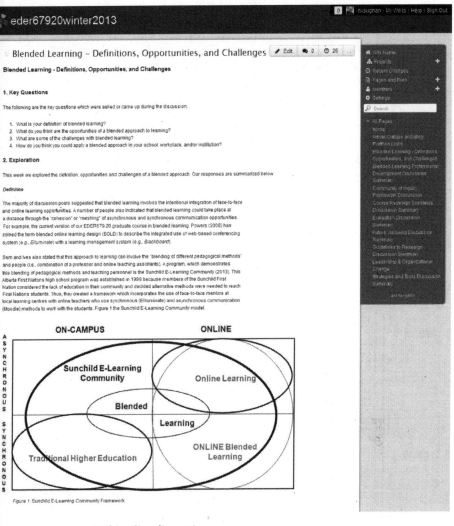

Blended Learning – Definitions, Opportunities, and Challenges ✎ Edit ● 0 ⊘ 26

Blended Learning - Definitions, Opportunities, and Challenges

1. Key Questions

The following are the key questions which were asked or came up during the discussion.

1. What is your definition of blended learning?
2. What do you think are the opportunities of a blended approach to learning?
3. What are some of the challenges with blended learning?
4. How do you think you could apply a blended approach in your school, workplace, and/or institution?

2. Exploration

This week we explored the definition, opportunities and challenges of a blended approach. Our responses are summarized below

Definition

The majority of discussion posts suggested that blended learning involves the intentional integration of face-to-face and online learning opportunities. A number of people also indicated that blended learning could take place at a distance through the "cohesion" or "meshing" of asynchronous and synchronous communication opportunities. For example, the current version of our EDER679.20 graduate course in blended learning. Powers (2008) has coined the term blended online learning design (BOLD) to describe the integrated use of web-based conferencing system (e.g., Elluminate) with a learning management system (e.g., Blackboard).

Sam and Ivea also stated that this approach to learning can involve the "blending of different pedagogical methods" and people (i.e., combination of a professor and online teaching assistants). A program, which demonstrates this blending of pedagogical methods and teaching personnel is the Sunchild E-Learning Community (2013). This Alberta First Nations high school program was established in 1999 because members of the Sunchild First Nation considered the lack of education in their community and decided alternative methods were needed to reach First Nations students. Thus, they created a framework which incorporates the use of face-to-face mentors at local learning centres with online teachers who use synchronous (Elluminate) and asynchronous communication (Moodle) methods to work with the students. Figure 1 the Sunchild E-Learning Community model.

Figure 1. Sunchild E-Learning Community Framework

FIGURE 6.3. Wiki online discussion summary

Students can easily edit and revise each other's work without software or computer platform compatibility issues (e.g., Mac versus PC). The finished product can then be exported in a variety of formats (e.g., PDF, Word, and html) and submitted for either peer or instructor assessment.

COURSE WIKI TEXTBOOKS

The potential also exists for students to use wikis to co-create course textbooks. There are numerous examples of such textbooks on the Wikibooks site. Wiki textbooks can be created and developed in a variety of ways. For example, student groups can be assigned to develop new chapters of the book while other groups can be given the task to peer review and edit existing book chapters.

SOCIAL NETWORKING

Social networking systems (SNS) allow users to share ideas, activities, events, and interests within their own individual networks. This can lead to the development of online communities of people who share common interests and activities. In blended learning courses, applications such as Facebook and LinkedIn can be used for study groups and online discussion board activities.

STUDY GROUPS

A number of educational research studies have been conducted over the years that have clearly demonstrated that, regardless of the subject matter, students working in small groups tend to learn more of what is taught and retain it longer than when the same content is presented in other instructional formats (Beckman, 1990; Chickering & Gamson, 1991; Johnson, Johnson, & Smith, 1991; McKeachie, Pintrich, Lin, & Smith, 1986). Many of the students in higher education today commute to campus and are therefore challenged to find the time and the location to work in study groups outside of class time. Recent studies by the EDUCAUSE Applied Centre for Research (Smith, Salaway & Borreson Caruso, 2010) and the Pew Internet & American Life Project (Lenhart, Purcell, Smith & Zickuhr, 2010) have indicated that Facebook is currently the most popular social networking system in higher education and that a number of students have begun using this application to support virtual study groups.

The study group application in Facebook allows students to post messages, conduct discussions, and exchange files. The advantage of using these group areas is that students can support each other, academically and socially, outside of class time. The downside of using Facebook is that this application is designed to promote social interaction rather than to create a learning space.

ONLINE DISCUSSION BOARD

As mentioned previously, online discussion forums can be used as a powerful catalyst to promote individual reflection and critical dialogue, outside of class time. Often, institutional learning management systems (LMS) such as Blackboard are used to support these discussions. These institutional applications often present collaborative challenges as it can be difficult to have external guests participate in the discussions (e.g., have to get an IT administrator to enrol guests in the LMS) and to provide students with moderator (e.g., instructor) status. Social networking tools such as Facebook and LinkedIn can be used to overcome these issues by creating a course group space (Figure 6.4).

The membership of groups in Facebook can be open or controlled by the moderator (e.g., course instructor). Anyone who has a Facebook account can be invited to become a member and participate in the online discussions. This could include past student members of the course (e.g., alumni), external experts, and even parents. Any member of the group can moderate the group discussion forums, and when a posting is made to the discussion, the person's Facebook profile image also appears, helping to create a more immediate sense of community.

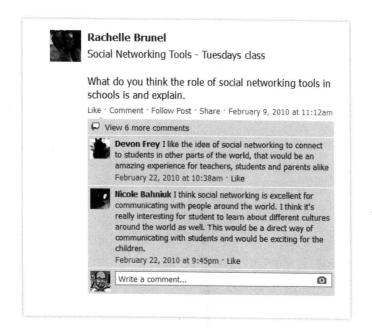

FIGURE 6.4. Student moderated online discussion forum in Facebook

SOCIAL CONTENT

Social content tools allow for the creation and exchange of user-generated content (e.g., text, audio, images, and video). Applications such as YouTube, Flikr, SlideShare, and PodOmatic provide a wealth of reusable media resources for learners and educators. These resources can be used to support pre-class activities, course learning objects, individual presentations, and group workshops.

Teachers and students can both use social content tools to create, post, and share digital learning objects before a class session. For example, teachers can use podcasts (e.g., PodOmatic), narrated MS PowerPoint presentations (e.g., SlideShare, Adobe Presenter) or video (e.g., YouTube) to communicate course concepts, scenarios, and case studies with students before class time. The advantages of using these types of learning objects are that they allow students to listen and view course-related material outside of class time, at their own pace, and as often as required to gain understanding (see Figure 6.5).

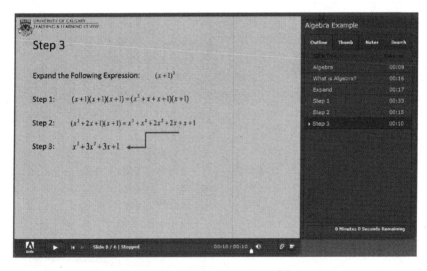

FIGURE 6.5. Narrated mathematical problem solving exercise

LEARNING OBJECTS

Students can also use social content applications to create learning objects to describe and explain threshold course concepts. For example, individuals or groups of students can be assigned the task of creating images, short podcasts, or YouTube video clips about key terms, definitions, or concepts related to the course. These resources can then be posted to the course website or linked to a learning object repository such as the Multimedia Educational Resource for Learning and Online Teaching (MERLOT) site (http://www.merlot.org/merlot/index.htm). The learning objects linked to MERLOT are categorized by discipline, and many of these objects have also been peer-reviewed by user communities with suggestions on how to use these digital resources in course assignments.

INDIVIDUAL PRESENTATIONS AND GROUP WORKSHOPS

Individual presentations and group workshops are often an essential part of a blended learning course. Unfortunately, these activities often focus on information dissemination (e.g., lecturing) rather than on discussion, and they can also consume a tremendous amount of precious class time. In order to avoid these issues, a number of instructors have begun to require students to use various social content tools to create narrated versions of their individual or group presentations.

These narrated presentations can then be posted or linked to an online discussion forum where other students are required to view and comment on them before a class or synchronous session (e.g., narrated PowerPoint presentations and YouTube videos). Class time is then used to discuss and debate the questions and issues raised in the discussion forum about the presentations.

MASHUPS

Mashup tools allow nontechnical users to mix or "mash" different types of data in order to discover new meanings or simply to present information in an unconventional format. For example, music mashups consist of mixing tracks from two or more different source songs. Mashup applications can be used for mapping and data visualization activities, presentation of student project and research work, analysis of class and online discussions, as well as digital storytelling.

ANALYSIS OF CLASS AND ONLINE DISCUSSIONS

As mentioned previously, many students in higher education are now bringing laptop computers and mobile devices into the classroom. By using wiki applications such as TitanPad, these tools can be used to take collaborative class notes. These notes can then be copied and pasted into a mashup application such as Wordle in order to create "word clouds" (Figure 6.6).

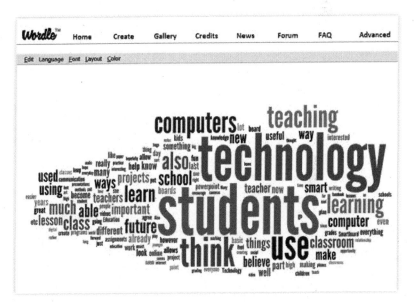

FIGURE 6.6. Class brainstorm results displayed in Wordle

Word clouds can be very useful for helping students identify key themes related to course concepts and issues. For example, at the beginning of a class, an instructor can ask the students to brainstorm what they already know about a course concept in Google Docs. The instructor copies and pastes this text into Wordle in order to create a word cloud. Higher-frequency words and phrases are displayed in a different colour and larger font size. The instructor can then facilitate a discussion about these key words and phrases and explain how they relate to a particular course concept.

This activity can also be repeated at the end of a class period or course module in order to demonstrate student changes in conceptual understanding. The instructor displays the word clouds created at the beginning and end of a class period and then asks students to compare and contrast the key words in an online discussion forum, after a class session. Conversely, an instructor can create word clouds from the discussion forum postings on a particular topic and then display these for further debate in a classroom session.

DIGITAL STORYTELLING

A series of mashup applications have been developed for both Mac (e.g., GarageBand, iMovie) and PC (e.g., Photo Story, Movie Maker) computers that allow users to combine and mix images, text, music, and video in order to create a digital story. Students can complete these stories individually or in groups and combine various forms of media, allowing for multiple pathways of creativity and success.

A number of websites have been developed to help students create their own digital stories. We highly recommend the University of Houston's Educational Uses of Digital Storytelling site (http://digitalstorytelling.coe.uh.edu/) as it provides examples, tools, tutorials, and rubrics for assessing digital stories.

SYNCHRONOUS COMMUNICATION AND CONFERENCING

The use of synchronous communication tools (e.g., text messaging, audio, and video) is becoming common in higher education. Some instructors are using these applications to replace classrooms sessions (e.g., online blended learning approach) while students are using these tools to support real-time collaborative project-based work.

SYNCHRONOUS CLASSROOM SESSIONS

At many institutions, synchronous communication applications such as Adobe Connect and Blackboard Collaborate have been integrated into the learning management system (Figure 6.7).

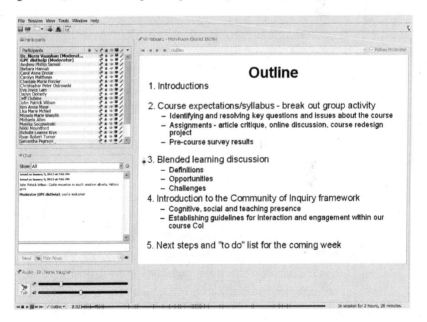

FIGURE 6.7. A Blackboard Collaborate session

Instructors can use these tools to create learning resources (e.g., record a mini-lecture, including diagrams and illustrations, in the accompanying whiteboard), host external guest presentations during class time, and/or replace physical classroom sessions with virtual ones. The focus of these sessions should not be on information transmission such as lecturing, but instead, be used to diagnose student misconceptions, foster critical dialogue, and support peer instruction.

STUDENT GROUP WORK

Students can also use synchronous applications such as Skype and WizIQ to communicate, collaborate, and co-construct projects and research papers in real-time. Because many of today's students in higher education commute to campuses, the advantage of using synchronous tools is that they can work together, anytime, anywhere they have a computer and a reasonable Internet connection. Some of these tools (e.g., Blackboard Collaborate) also allow the students to share desktop applications and to record their sessions in case a group member is absent.

VIRTUAL WORLDS

Virtual world applications such as Second Life, Croquet, and The Palace allow for synchronous interaction in 3-D immersive worlds. These tools support collaborative and creative project-based work that goes beyond text-based and audio communication. Many campus-based learning activities such as lectures, tutorials, and labs can be replicated and enhanced in a virtual world application (Figure 6.8).

For example, students can take part in virtual role-plays, simulations, and experiments. They can visit educational "islands" where they can receive mentorship and advice from resident experts (e.g.,

NASA). Students can also visit foreign islands where they can learn about different languages and cultures.

FIGURE 6.8. Students meeting for a virtual class in Second Life

FUTURE TRENDS IN TECHNOLOGY

Predicting the future is challenging in any context and potentially even more unproductive in terms of technology and its possible applications. For this reason we shall focus on identifiable trends that in the near future will most likely continue to shape educational practice significantly as it relates to blended learning.

The first and perhaps most significant trend is the adoption of collaborative approaches to teaching and learning in higher education. This involves much more than simply interacting and sharing information. Collaboration involves a purposeful partnering of students and instructors to solve relevant problems. It provides an environment to test conceptions and validate personally constructed knowledge.

The second trend is the recognition that through the adoption of social media applications, communities can be created and sustained over time and place. Brown and Adler (2008) suggest that this will lead to "learning 2.0" environments, which go "beyond providing free access to traditional course materials and educational tools and create a participatory architecture for supporting communities of learners" (p. 28).

The third trend is the ability of social media tools to support diverse educational purposes, approaches, and audiences. This provides students with multiple pathways for success in blended learning courses. While we can identify trends and even principles of practice, the decentralization of the teaching and learning process will inevitably lead to greater diversity and opportunities to learn. The choice of what and how to learn can only be a plus for educators and students.

As opportunities for interaction and collaboration increase through the proliferation of social media technologies, more pressure will be placed on educational institutions to adopt collaborative–constructivist approaches that engage learners in communities of inquiry. Collaborative learning goes beyond passively sharing information. For this reason, social media technologies will have a transformative influence in both formal and informal learning environments.

CONCLUSION

The historical ideal of higher education has been to learn in collaborative communities of inquiry (Lipman, 1991). This chapter has demonstrated the potential of using social media technologies and educational strategies to recapture this vision, even in large introductory undergraduate courses. The key is to redesign our blended learning courses for active and collaborative learning experiences that enable students to take responsibility for their learning and validate their understanding through discourse and debate with their peers.

7 Conclusion

We still educate our students based on an agricultural timetable, in
an industrial setting, but tell students they live in a digital age.
(US Department of Education, 2005, p. 22)

INTRODUCTION

Adoption of the Community of Inquiry principles, which we have
explored in this book, is inherently transformational. They represent a new educational paradigm that will be extremely disruptive to
those higher educational institutions heavily invested in information dissemination. The CoI paradigm represents significant change
— change that better maps onto the needs of a connected knowledge
society. It is an approach to teaching and learning that distances
itself from the traditional practices of dispensing information either
through a lecture or self-study materials. New paradigms such as

the CoI framework have drawn attention as a result of enormous information and technological advancements.

> Today's technological revolution, with its order of magnitude advances that have left little of common life unchanged, presents an open challenge to the University to once again "reinvent" itself. Indeed, it could be argued that the pressure for change placed on the University today is greater than any it has faced in any previous historical epoch. (Amirault & Visser, 2009, p. 64)

The nature and rate of change in society associated with new and emerging information and communications technology represents an enormous adaptation challenge for education. This may be the most significant challenge facing higher education. In particular, this challenge is the adoption of appropriate information and communications technology in the classroom. New and emerging social media technologies are the catalyst for rethinking what we are doing in higher education classrooms. Keeping in mind that technology is only a means to an end (as powerful as it is), we must be clear about our educational goals.

We have argued that blended learning in a community of inquiry context provides a coherent way forward that can capitalize on the structural changes in society. Blended learning provides a thoughtful adoption of communications technologies that can address the challenges of providing more engaged learning experiences in higher education. Once we understand how best to integrate technology in the form of blended learning, we must understand how to lead and manage this inevitable transformation. The key is to guide this inevitable change with awareness and purpose. How we will implement these technologies and define our educational goals must be a collaborative effort.

Education by its inherent nature is a purposeful and collaborative enterprise. This has been made clear in the previous chapters. However, the interdependency of the educational community is not often recognized or practiced when it comes to leadership. One of the great deficiencies of the higher education system is the lack of substantive collaboration in establishing a vision, developing strategic action plans and, most importantly, implementing these plans in a sustainable manner. Collaborative leadership instils common purpose, trust, and identification with the institution. These are the principles associated with a community of inquiry that are relevant to higher education leadership. Planning for open communication and reflective discourse, establishing community and purposeful inquiry, and ensuring meaningful resolutions and applications form the template for collaborative leadership. This goes well beyond charisma and public persona. It means working hard behind the scenes to bring people together focused on meaningful change.

Higher educational institutions generally have not shown a commitment to change that is inevitably disruptive. While information and communications technologies (ICT) are being adopted in the classroom, educational leaders have not yet grasped the full significance of the impending changes. A vision must be informed by the appropriate set of principles. Unfortunately, most leaders are not prepared to spend the commensurate time understanding the paradigmatic shift that is upon us, particularly with regard to undergraduate education. We have to ask: To what extent does senior leadership understand engaged inquiry approaches to learning and the impact of information and communications technology in realizing the ideals of higher education? It is to this point that we raise the issue of collaborative leadership required to bring higher education into the connected knowledge age.

Too often leaders hold to views about teaching and learning that are simply at odds with technological developments in the larger society. Current classroom practices are not sustainable. Leaders must focus more of their attention on matters of teaching and learning and engage in a collaborative, open, and sustained commitment to create active learning communities using the same principles that are the foundation of a CoI. The change that we have described and discussed involves significant technological change but this is simply a means to an end. The real argument is to what purpose is the change directed.

To date, the focus has been on the adoption of technology for administrative services. This investment has failed to reach the classroom in any appreciable manner. Senior administrators do not fully appreciate the effect technology is having on learning and the need to reshape what we do in the classroom. This is not a direct criticism of leadership. Understanding collaborative approaches as reflected in a community of inquiry combined with the complex possibilities of a blended learning design is an enormous demand on senior leadership. However, leaders must be prepared to question conventional classroom practices and to become engaged in and committed to the transformation of approaches to teaching and learning in a digital society. Senior administrators must be participants in digital designs for creating and sustaining communities of inquiry. The challenge is to understand their role.

Collaborative leadership is neither top-down nor bottom-up. It is the fusion of both, just as collaborative constructivist approaches to learning are the fusion of sage on the stage and guide on the side. Collaborative leadership is the rejection of such dualisms and the creation of a unified purpose and effort. Leaders must display characteristics that reflect openness and courage. The lessons of the past have shown us that leadership too often succumbs to insecurity and surrounds itself with sycophants. Its other failing is in avoiding the need for fundamental change and embellishing insignificant change through extensive public relations initiatives that choose rhetoric over reality. Vision and insight are developed through a deep understanding of the organization and its challenges, and most importantly, they must be informed through sustained collaboration. When vision and courage intersect, real commitment and actual change result.

Leadership also requires sustained commitment and honest feedback. Commitment to assessment and appropriate adjustments over time are at the heart of real change. This means honest and relevant feedback with regard to the strategic vision. It means a critical focus on the progress being made to achieve the strategic vision and actions that can improve outcomes. Inevitably there will be different values and interests that can only be resolved through dialogue. Only through sustained collaborative action over a significant period of time will institutional change be realized.

The kind of change that we have addressed in this book is transformational. It is fair to say that there is a lack of strategic focus and commitment with regard to the need to transform teaching and learning. It has been argued that much of this can be attributed to what Ginsberg (2011) refers to as the "all-administrative university" (p.197) and how it has grown and isolated the leaders from the purpose of higher education: the learning experience. Higher education requires transformed classroom approaches and organizational structures to initiate and sustain these changes. If there is to be an efficient paradigm shift, resources will have to be shifted from administrative purposes to changes in the classroom. There is growing evidence that the leadership and structure of successful higher educational institutions will need to be transformed if they are to realize the full potential of blended learning in a collaborative constructivist paradigm. The key to the transformation of teaching and learning that we have explored in this book will depend largely on a commitment to collaborative leadership and governance structure. Everybody must be onboard.

Blended learning course:
Introductory survey question examples

The purpose of this survey is to provide us with a shared understanding of our backgrounds, computer experience, goals, and expectations for this blended learning course.

1. Gender
   ☐ Female
   ☐ Male

2. Age
   ☐ 15–19
   ☐ 20–25
   ☐ 26–30
   ☐ 31 plus

3. Employment status
   ☐ I have a full-time job.
   ☐ I have a part-time job.
   ☐ I am not presently working.

4. Previous experience with digital technology tools and applications. Please select as many items as applicable.

☐ I own a SMART phone (e.g., cell phone with Internet access).

☐ I have a blog.

☐ I have a Twitter account.

☐ I have a Facebook account.

☐ I have a YouTube account.

☐ I have a Second Life account.

☐ I have my own laptop.

5. Personal rating of computer skills

☐ Novice (not really comfortable using computers)

☐ Intermediate (comfortable using a computer)

☐ Advanced (have developed some expertise and enjoy using a computer)

6. Home Internet access

☐ Yes

☐ No

7. Course goals

What are your goals for this course? What do you want to take away from this blended learning course experience?

8. Weekly class sessions
   What do you expect will happen during the weekly class sessions? What will the instructor do in class and what will you do?

   ```
   
   
   
   
   
   ```

9. Outside of class work expectations
   What type of work do you expect to do outside of the classroom for this course, if any?

   ```
   
   
   
   
   ```

10. Assessment of learning
    How do you think your learning in this course will be assessed?

    ```
    
    
    
    
    ```

References

Akyol, Z., & Garrison, D. R. (2008). The development of a community of inquiry over time in an online course: Understanding the progression and integration of social, cognitive and teaching presence. *Journal of Asynchronous Learning Networks, 12*(3), 3–22.

Akyol, Z., Vaughan, N., & Garrison, D. R. (2011). The impact of course duration on the development of a community of inquiry. *Interactive Learning Environments, 19*(3), 231–246.

Akyol, Z., & Garrison, D. R. (2011a). Assessing metacognition in an online community of inquiry. *Internet & Higher Education, 14*(3), 183–190.

Akyol, Z., & Garrison, D. R. (2011b). Learning and satisfaction in online communities of inquiry. In S. B. Eom & J. B. Arbaugh (Eds.), *Student satisfaction and learning outcomes in e-learning: An introduction to empirical research* (pp. 23–35). Hershey, PA: Information Science.

Akyol, Z., & Garrison, D. R. (2011c). Understanding cognitive presence in an online and blended community of inquiry: Assessing outcomes and processes for deep approaches to learning. *British Journal of Educational Technology, 42*(2), 233–250.

Alverno College. (2001). *Assessment essentials: Definition of terms.* Available online at: http://depts.alverno.edu/saal/terms.html

American Association of Higher Education and Accreditation. (1996). *Nine principles of good practice for assessing student learning.* Available online at: http://www.niu.edu/assessment/Manual/_docs/9Principles.pdf

Amirault, R. J., & Visser, Y. L. (2009). The university in periods of technological change: A historically grounded perspective. *Journal of Computing in Higher Education, 21*(1), 62–79.

Arbaugh, J. B. (2008). Does the community of inquiry framework predict outcomes in online MBA courses? *International Review of Research in Open and Distance Learning, 9*, 1–21.

Arbaugh, J. B., Cleveland-Innes, M., Diaz, S. R., Garrison, D. R., Ice, P., Richardson, J.C, & Swan, K. P. (2008). Developing a community of inquiry instrument: Testing a measure of the community of inquiry framework using a multi-institutional sample. *The Internet and Higher Education, 11*(3–4), 133–136.

Barkley, E. F. (2009). *Student engagement techniques: A handbook for college faculty*. San Francisco, CA: Jossey-Bass.

Beckman, M. (1990). Collaborative learning: Preparation for the workplace and democracy. *College Teaching, 38*(4), 128–133.

Bierly, P. E., Stark, E. M., & Kessler, E. H. (2009). The moderating effects of virtuality on the antecedents and outcome of NPD team trust. *Journal of Product Innovation Management, 26*, 551–565.

Biggs, J. (1998). Assumptions underlying new approaches to assessment. In P. Stimson & P. Morris (Eds.), *Curriculum and assessment in Hong Kong: Two components, one system*, (pp. 351–384). Hong Kong: Open University of Hong Kong Press.

Bonk, C., Kim, K., & Zeng, X. (2004). Future directions of blended learning in higher education and workplace learning settings. In C. J. Bonk & C. R. Graham, C. R. (Eds.), *Handbook of blended learning: Global perspectives, local designs* (pp. 550–568). San Francisco, CA: John Wiley.

Boston, W., Diaz, S. R., Gibson, A., Ice, P., Richardson, J., & Swan, K. (2009). An exploration of the relationship between indicators of the community of inquiry framework and retention in online programs. *Journal of Asynchronous Learning Networks, 13*(3), 67–83.

Boud, D. (2000). Sustainable assessment: Rethinking assessment for the learning society. *Studies in Continuing Education, 22*(2), 151–167.

Brown, J. S., & Adler, R. P. (2008). Minds on fire: Open education, the long tail, and learning 2.0. *EDUCAUSE Review*, 17–32.

Chickering, A. W., & Gamson, Z. F. (1987). Seven principles of good practice in undergraduate education. *American Association for Higher Education Bulletin, 39* (March), 3–7.

Chickering, A. W., & Gamson, Z. F. (Eds.). (1991). Applying the seven principles for good practice in undergraduate education. *New Directions for Teaching and Learning, 47*. San Francisco: Jossey-Bass.

Cleveland-Innes, M., & Emes, C. (2005). Social and academic interaction in higher education contexts and the effect on deep learning. *National Association of Student Personnel Administrators Journal, 42*(2), 241-262.

Cleveland-Innes, M., & Garrison, D. R. (2009). The role of learner in an online community of inquiry: Instructor support for first-time online learners. In N. Karacapilidis (Ed.), *Solutions and innovations in web-based technologies for augmented learning: Improved platforms, tools and applications*. Hershey, PA: IGI Global.

Cleveland-Innes, M., & Garrison, D. R. (2011). Higher education and post-industrial society: New ideas about teaching, learning, and technology. In L. Moller & J. Huett (Eds.), *The next generation of distance education: Unconstrained learning*. New York: Springer.

Cleveland-Innes, M., Garrison, R., & Kinsel, E. (2008). The role of learner in an online community of inquiry: Responding to the challenges of first-time online learners. In N. Karacapilidis (Ed.), *Solutions and innovations in web-based technologies for augmented learning: Improved platforms, tools and applications.* Hersey, PA: IGI Global.

Clifford, P., Friesen, S., & Lock, J. (2004). *Coming to teach in the 21st century: A research study conducted by the Galileo Education Network for Alberta Learning.* Available online from: http://www.galileo.org/research/publications/ctt.pdf

Crouch, C. H., & Mazur, E. (2001). Peer instruction: Ten years of experience and results. *American Journal of Physics, 69*(9), 970–977.

Downes, S. (2004). Educational blogging. *EDUCAUSE Review, 39*(5), 14–26.

Dziuban, C. D., Moskal, P. D., Bradford, G. R., Brophy-Ellison, J., & Groff, A. T. (2010). Constructs that impact the net generation's satisfaction with online learning. In R. Sharpe, H. Beetham, & S. De Freitas (Eds.), *Rethinking learning for a digital age: How learners are shaping their own experiences.* New York, NY: Routledge.

Entwistle, N. J. (2000). Approaches to studying and levels of understanding: The influences of teaching and assessment. In J. C. Smart (Ed.), *Higher education: Handbook of theory and research, XV* (pp. 156–218). New York: Agathon.

Entwistle, N., & Tait, H. (1990). Approaches to learning, evaluations of teaching, and preferences for contrasting academic environments. *Higher Education, 19,* (169–194).

Eom, S. (2006). The role of instructors as a determinant of students' satisfaction in university online education. In *Proceedings of the Sixth IEEE International Conference on Advanced Learning Technologies – ICALT* (985–988). Washington, DC: IEEE Computer Society.

Foundation Coalition. (2002). *Peer assessment and peer evaluation.* Available online at: http://www.foundationcoalition.org/publications/brochures/2002peer_assessment.pdf

Galileo Educational Network. (2011). *What is inquiry?* Available online at: http://www.galileo.org/inquiry-what.html

Garrison, D. R. (2011). *E-learning in the 21st century: A framework for research and practice* (2nd ed.). London, UK: Routledge/Falmer.

Garrison, D. R., Anderson, T., & Archer, W. (2000). Critical thinking in a text-based environment: Computer conferencing in higher education. Internet and Higher Education, 11(2), 1–14.

Garrison, D. R., Anderson, T., & Archer, W. (2001). Critical thinking, cognitive presence and computer conferencing in distance education. *American Journal of Distance Education, 15*(1), 7–23.

Garrison, D. R., & Cleveland-Innes, M. (2005). Facilitating cognitive presence in online learning: Interaction is not enough. *American Journal of Distance Education, 19*(3), 133–148.

Garrison, D. R., Cleveland-Innes, M., & Fung, T. (2010). Exploring causal relationships among cognitive, social and teaching presence: Student perceptions of the community of inquiry framework. *The Internet and Higher Education, 13*(1–2), 31–36.

Garrison, D. R., & Vaughan, N. (2008). *Blended learning in higher education.* San Francisco: Jossey-Bass.

Geerdink, C. (2012, June 26). Learning to know: It's all about curiousity. (Web log comment). Available online at: http://www.neth-er.eu/en/news/learning-know-it%E2%80%99s-all-about-curiosity

Gibbs, G. (2006). How assessment frames student learning. In C. Bryan & K. Clegg (Eds.), *Innovative assessment in higher education* (pp. 23–36). London, UK: Routledge.

Gibbs, G., & Simpson, C. (2004). Conditions under which assessment supports students' learning. *Learning and Teaching in Higher Education, 1,* 3–31.

Ginsberg, B. (2011). *The fall of the faculty: The rise of the all-administrative university and why it matters.* New York: Oxford University Press.

Gorsky, P., Caspi, A., and Trumper, R. (2006). Campus-based university students' use of dialogue. *Studies in Higher Education, 31*(1), 71–87.

Hadjerrouit S. (2008). Towards a blended learning model for teaching and learning computer programming: A case study. *Informatics in Education, 7*(2), 181–210.

Hattie, J. (2009). Visible learning: A synthesis of over 800 meta-analyses relating to achievement. New York: Routledge.

Hedberg, J., & Corrent-Agostinho, S. (1999). Creating a postgraduate virtual community: Assessment drives learning. In B. Collis & R. Oliver (Eds.), *Proceedings of World Conference on Educational Multimedia, Hypermedia and Telecommunications.* (pp. 1093–1098). AACE: Chesapeake, VA. Available online at: http://www.editlib.org/p/7040

Ice, P., Curtis, R., Phillips, P., & Wells, J. (2007). Using asynchronous audio feedback to enhance teaching presence and students' sense of community. *Journal of Asynchronous Learning Networks, 11*(2), 3–25.

Johnson, D. W., Johnson, R. T., & Smith, K. A. (1991). Cooperative learning: Increasing college faculty instructional productivity. *ASHE–FRIC Higher Education Report No. 4.* Washington, D.C.: School of Education and Human Development, George Washington University.

Johnson, L., Levine, A., Smith, R., & Stone, S. (2010). The 2010 horizon report. Austin, TX: The New Media Consortium. Available online at: www.nmc.org/pdf/2010-Horizon-Report.pdf

Joubert, J. (1983). *The notebooks of Joseph Joubert.* (P. Auster, Ed. & Trans.). New York: North Point Press. (Original work published in 1842.)

Kanuka, H. (2005). An exploration into facilitating higher levels of learning in a text-based Internet learning environment using diverse instructional strategies. *Journal of Computer-Mediated Communication, 10*(3), article 8. Available online at: http://jcmc.indiana.edu/vol10/issue3/kanuka.html

Kaplan, A. M., & Haenlein, M. (2010). Users of the world, unite! The challenges and opportunities of social media. *Business Horizons, 53*(1), 59–68.

Keen, A. (2007). *The cult of the amateur: How today's Internet is killing our culture.* New York: Doubleday.

Keller, G. (2008). *Higher education and the new society.* Baltimore, MA: Johns Hopkins University Press.

Knowles, M. S. (1986). *Using learning contracts.* San Francisco: Jossey-Bass.

Kuh, G. D., Kinzie, J., Scuh, J. H., Whitt, E. J., & Associates (2005). *Student success in college.* San Francisco: Jossey-Bass.

Lenhart, A., Purcell, K., Smith. A., & Zickuhr, K. (2010). *Social media and mobile internet use among teens and young adults.* Washington, D.C.: Pew Internet & American Life Project.

Leuf, B., & Cunningham, W. (2001). *The wiki way: Quick collaboration on the web.* New York: Addison-Wesley.

Lipman, M. (1991). *Thinking in education.* Cambridge: Cambridge University Press.

Lipman, M. (2003). *Thinking in education* (2nd ed.). Cambridge: Cambridge University Press.

Marton, F., & Saljo, R. (1984) Approaches to learning. In F. Marton, D. Hounsell, & N. Entwistle (Eds.), *The experience of learning,* Edinburgh: Scottish Academic Press.

McKeachie, W. J., Pintrich, P. R., Lin, Y. G., & Smith, D. A. F. (1986). *Teaching and learning in the college classroom: A review of the research literature.* Ann Arbor, MI: National Center for Research to Improve Postsecondary Teaching and Learning, University of Michigan.

Nicol, D. J., & Macfarlane-Dick, D. (2006). Formative assessment and self-regulated learning: A model and seven principles of good feedback practice. *Studies in Higher Education, 31*(2), 199–218.

Novak, G. M., Patterson, E. T., Gavrin, A. D., & Christian, W. (1999). *Just-in-time teaching: Blending active learning with web technology*. Upper Saddle River, NJ: Prentice Hall.

O'Reilly, T. (2005). *What is web 2.0: Design patterns and business models for the next generation of software*. Available online at: http://oreilly.com/web2/archive/what-is-web-20.html

Ouimet, J. A., & Smallwood, R. A. (2005). CLASSE—the class-level survey of student engagement. *Assessment Update, 17*(6), 13-15.

Pask, G. (1976). *Conversation theory: Applications in education and epistemology*. Amsterdam: Elsevier.

Pelz, B. (2004). (My) three principles of effective online pedagogy. *Journal of Asynchronous Learning Networks, 8*(3), 33–46.

Perry, W. G., Jr. (1981). Cognitive and ethical growth: The making of meaning. In A. W. Chickering, *The modern American college* (pp. 76–116). San Francisco: Jossey-Bass.

Pond, W. K. (2002, Summer). Distributed education in the 21st century: Implications for quality assurance. *Online Journal of Distance Learning Administration, 5*(2). Available online at: http://www.westga.edu/~distance/ojdla/summer52/pond52.html

Ramsden, P. (2003). *Learning to teach in higher education* (2nd ed.). London Series in Educational Innovation: Routledge.

Rensselaer Polytechnic Institute. (1996). *Clay Patrick Bedford*. Available online at: http://www.rpi.edu/about/hof/bedford.html

Rowntree, D. (1977). *Assessing students*. London: Harper & Row.

Shea, P., & Bidjerano, T. (2009). Cognitive presence and online learner engagement: A cluster analysis of the community of inquiry framework. *Journal of Computing in Higher Education, 21*, 199–217.

Shea, P., Li, C. S., Swan, K., & Pickett, A. (2005). Developing learning community in online asynchronous college courses: The role of teaching presence. *The Journal of Asynchronous Learning Networks 9*(4), 59–82.

Sitzman, T., Ely, K., Brown, K. G., & Bauer, K. N. (2010). Adding a web-based perspective to the self-assessment of knowledge: Compelling reasons to utilize affective measures of learning. *Academy of Management Learning & Education, 9*(2), 169–191.

Smith, S., Salaway, G., & Borreson Caruso, J. (2009). *The ECAR study of undergraduate students and information technology, 2009: Key findings*. Boulder, CO: EDUCAUSE Center for Applied Research.

Teaching, Learning, and Technology (TLT) Group. (2011). *Rubrics: Definition, tools, examples, references*. Available online at: http://www.tltgroup.org/resources/flashlight/rubrics.htm

Team-Based Learning Collaborative. (2011). *Getting started with TBL*. Available online at: http://www.teambasedlearning.org/

Thistlethwaite, J. (2006). More thoughts on 'assessment drives learning'. *Medical Education, 40*(11), 1149–1150.

Tinney, J. (2013). A senior administrator's view of technology and learning. *Education Canada, 53*(4), Available online at: http://www.cea-ace.ca/education-canada/article/senior-administrator%E2%80%99s-view-technology-and-learning

US Department of Education. (2005). *Toward a new golden age in American education: How the Internet, the law, and today's students are revolutionizing expectations*. Washington: USDE.

Vaughan, N. D. (2008). The use of wikis and weblogs to support deep approaches to learning. *The University College of Fraser Valley Research Review, 1*(3), 47–60. Available online at: http://journals.ucfv.ca/rr/RR13/article-PDFs/6-vaughan.pdf

Vaughan, N. D. (2010a). A blended community of inquiry approach: Linking student engagement to course redesign. *Internet and Higher Education, 13*(1–2), 60–65.

Vaughan, N. D. (2010b). *How can students improve their academic course work through the use of interactive learning technologies?* Paper presented at the 2010 Canadian Society for Studies in Education (CSSE) Conference.

Yeh, S. S. (2009). The cost-effectiveness of raising teacher quality. *Educational Research Review, 4*(3), 220–232.

Index

affective expression, 57

assessment (*see also* self-assessment): design of, 33; of inquiry study, 69; by instructor, 91–94; and learning contracts, 71–72; of participation, 32, 40; of peers, 87–91; principles of, 82–83; student/teacher views of, 81–82; tied to critical thinking, 41–42; triad-approach to, 94–95

asynchronous communication: advantages of, 39–40, 41; and assessment, 93–94; and design, 24, 36–37; and facilitation, 47; importance of, 9; strategies for facilitating, 51, 52, 54

Blackboard, 26, 29, 88, 111, 118

blended learning: and assessment, 94–95; defined, 1, 8; described, 8–10; and facilitation, 45–46; and future of technology, 119–120, 122; introductory survey questions for, 127–129; need for, 2–3, 7; principles of, 3–4, 17–18

blogs, 60, 86, 89, 93, 104–106, 107

brainstorming, 40, 115

Classroom Survey of Student Engagement (CLASSE), 43

cognitive presence: design of, 34–44; and direct instruction, 64–65; direct instruction

strategies for, 75–79; as part of Community of Inquiry framework, 11–12; principles of, 54–55, 72–73; responsibility for, 14, 73–75; strategies for facilitating, 55–60

collaboration (*see also* Community of Inquiry (CoI)): assessment of, 42; and future of social media, 119–120; in inquiry-based project, 68–71; and interpersonal relationships, 66–67; as key to Community of Inquiry, 3, 99–100; and leadership, 123–125; and shift in higher education, 97–100; in strategies for facilitating cognitive presence, 55–60; synchronous applications of, 118

collaborative constructivism, 34, 125

committed relativism, 58

Community of Inquiry (CoI): and assessment principles, 83; and changing technology, 121–122; and collaboration, 3, 99–100; design concerns, 19–21; and direct instruction, 64–65; and leadership, 123–125; principles of, 4, 17–18, 49; responsibilities of direct instruction in, 73–75; Survey, 43; theoretical framework for, 10–15

course evaluation, 43

course textbooks, 110
critical thinking: activities for,
38–39; and assessment,
41–42; and cognitive presence,
36, 57–58; in inquiry-based
project rubric, 69–70; through
Community of Inquiry, 10

debates, 104
design. *see* instructional design
digital storytelling, 116
digital technologies, 69, 84–85,
87–91, 92–95
direct instruction: in delivery
of cognitive presence,
39; principle of cognitive
presence, 72–73; principle
of social presence, 65–67;
responsibilities for cognitive
presence, 73–75; role of, 47,
63–65; strategies for online
discussion, 75–79; strategies
for social presence, 68–71

engagement: and cognitive
presence, 41, 43, 54; and direct
instruction, 67; and guidelines
for online discussion, 30–31;
importance of, 9; modelling of,
32; and teaching presence, 47
expert assessment, 69, 70, 74, 93
exploration, 34, 36, 57–59, 69, 75,
79, 108

Facebook, 111–112
facilitation: and discussion,
31–33; importance of, 45–46;
integrating face-to-face with
online, 60–61; principles of,
48–49, 54–55; role of, 47–48;
strategies for facilitating
cognitive presence, 55–60;
strategies for facilitating social
presence, 50–54; techniques
for cognitive presence, 40–41

Galileo Educational Network,
68–71
Google Docs, 84, 88, 92
group cohesion: activities for, 27,
28; designing for, 25–26;
and direct instruction,
66–67; and facilitation by
instructor, 31–33; as focus at
beginning of inquiry process,
13; and guidelines for online
discussion, 30–31; strategies
for facilitating, 49, 50–54
group essays, 108
group projects, 26, 27, 28. *see also*
team–based learning

individual presentations, 114
inquiry (*see also* Community of
Inquiry (CoI)): and design of
cognitive presence, 34–44; as
focus of principles of practice,
4; as part of critical thinking,
10; practical model for, 75–76,
79, 102, 108; principle of, 54–
55; project rubric for, 68–71;
strategies for facilitating,
55–60
instructional design: of cognitive
presence, 34–44; planning
process of, 21–24; questions
and concerns about, 19–21; of
social presence, 24–33
instructor assessment, 91–95
integration, 9, 10–11, 60–61, 76,
79, 108
Internet, 20, 32. *see also* blogs;
social media; social
networking; wikis
interpersonal relationships, 25, 29,
49, 50, 66–67

journals, 75, 86–87, 89
Just-in-Time Teaching (JiTT),
102–103